THE AUDACITY OF GRACE:
FINDING GOD'SOLUTION TO LIFE'S PROBLEMS

STEPHEN BAWA

© **Copyright Stephen Bawa, 2024 - All rights reserved.**

The content within this book may not be reproduced, duplicated or transmitted without direct written permission from the author or the publisher.

Under no circumstances will any blame or legal responsibility be held against the publisher, or author, for any damages, reparation, or monetary loss due to the information contained within this book. Either directly or indirectly. You are responsible for your own choices, actions, and results.

Legal Notice:

This book is copyright protected. This book is only for personal use. You cannot amend, distribute, sell, use, quote or paraphrase any part, of the content within this book, without the consent of the author or publisher.

Disclaimer Notice:

Please note the information contained within this document is for educational and entertainment purposes only. All effort has been expended to present accurate, up-to-date, and reliable, complete information. No warranties of any kind are declared or implied. Readers acknowledge that the author is not engaging in the rendering of legal, financial, medical or professional advice. The content within this book has been derived from various sources. Please consult a licensed professional before attempting any techniques outlined in this book.

By reading this document, the reader agrees that under no circumstances is the author responsible for any losses, direct or indirect, which are incurred as a result of the use of the information contained within this document, including, but not limited to, — errors, omissions, or inaccuracies.

Published by Amazon
Book Cover designed by
Alex Tunde Adisa
Contact Stephen@tkm.one

This book is dedicated to my Lord Jesus Christ the Great Saviour and the Redeemer of the mankind, the Almighty God of Grace.

And

*To my late wife Dorothy May Bawa
A genuine Princess of the Kingdom who has gone to be with the Lord who she loved and served all her life.*

ACKNOWLEDGEMENTS

I would like to acknowledge the following people whose encouragement made this book possible to write. I want to place on record the immense contribution of my late wife, Dorothy May Bawa who was instrumental in encouraging me to write this book, but who although though saw the beginning of it, was called home to be with the Lord and regrettably never saw the final draft.

I would also like to thank my Sweetheart and new wife; Linda Joyce Bawa who was very kind in giving me time and space to complete the manuscript of this book and has patiently read and re-read the manuscript and has made very useful and positive comments.

I am very grateful to my very dear friend Dr Pastor Samuel Abiodun Goddy, a Scientist and a passionate servant of Jesus Christ who took time to go through the rough draft of the manuscript and tried to polish up its jumbled chapters.

I would like to thank my good friend Rev Dr John Clements, Pastor of the Old Meeting House Congregational Church; Norwich (founded by the Puritans in 1643) who in spite of his very busy schedule has taken time to undertake the heavy responsibility of proof-reading the manuscript of this book and by casting the Clergy man's eyes on the theological aspects of the narratives of the book.

I am thankful to my son and daughter in the Lord, Alex Tunde Adisa and his lovely wife Omolayo Adisa who laboured tirelessly to produce the graphics and the design of the cover and the back page of this book.

As the book contains entirely my Christian personal views, experience and understanding, I take a full responsibility for any inadequacies that may be contained in this book.

Stephen Bawa

The Kingdom Ministries

Stephen@tkm.one

CONTENTS

Endorsement by Pastor Dr Samuel Goddy	9
Forward by Rev Dr John Clements	13
Introduction	17
1. My Grace is Sufficient for You *2 Corinthians 12: 9*	21
2. The Audacity of Grace	37
3. The Practical Grace	71
4. Restarting Afresh with Grace	81
5. God has Plan for Your Life	91
6. Practical Christianity *Part 1*	97
7. Who are the Christians? *Part 1*	105
8. Who are the Christians? *Part 2*	111
9. Have Faith in God	117
10. What is Faith? *Part 2*	125
11. Trusting God with Your Problems	133
12. Prayer of Faith: The Weapon of Victory *Part 1*	143
13. How To Pray An Effective Prayer	153
14. Living for Christ *Part 1*	159
15. The Work of the Holy Spirit	163
16. Living the Word of God	169
17. The Importance of the Word of God	173
18. The Supremacy of Christ	179
19. Living the Kingdom Life	183
20. Whose Side Are You On? *Exodus 32: 26a*	189
Sinners Prayer	195

Appendix 197
About the Author 209

ENDORSEMENT BY PASTOR DR SAMUEL GODDY

The book 'Audacity of Grace' describes the grace and mercy of God which is free and available in abundance to anyone who can call on the name of the Lord in their hour of distress and trouble. No one, no matter how sinful is beyond the reach of the mercy of the Almighty God. God's approval is the deciding factor and with genuine obedience to the leading of the spirit of God which gives the instruction is the key. No one receives anything except through God's grace.

The book uses many biblical characters and their episodes in life they went through to illustrate this notion of God's 'grace is sufficient for you' - a statement accredited to Apostle Paul. God's grace was sufficient to see Paul through his weaknesses and ordeal and to make him triumphant in spite of many obstacles and sufferings he went through.

The Almighty God is the final arbiter and our Father is a God of integrity. In order for us his children to know what he is doing in our lives and to obtain mercy and grace in time of need, he invites us to boldly come to his throne of grace. It was this grace that Noah found for the Holy Spirit to bear witness to his moral uprightness and impeccable integrity whilst every man and woman of his days were steeped in sin and godlessness. Noah and his household were exempted when God wiped from the face of the earth all the living things he had created.

Human moral failings and weaknesses resulted in sexual temptation and sin for Samson and David. David did not die in shame like Samson. David's genuine repentance and full confession of his sin led to his forgiveness from God and restoration to favour and grace.

The greatest miracle in a Christian's life is the miracle of salvation which also takes place by grace. Also, to live a true Christian life, that is, to love the Lord Jesus Christ and keep his law is only by the grace of God.

Finally, as Christians, Jesus Christ our captain did not teach us a bed of roses. With the example of a set-back experienced by David and his men, this book teaches us to pursue to recover after inquiring from the Lord. David did not quit but turned to God, the source of limitless power, authority and strength. He encouraged himself in the Lord of his salvation. He called on God that never fails, a God that specialises in doing impossibilities, a wonder working God of ages. Here, David showed how he trusted in the Lord and made Him his first port of call.

ENDORSEMENT BY PASTOR DR SAMUEL GODDY

Our God is a God of second chances. Telling yourself and God that you are powerless is a sign of humility before God and acknowledging that only by His intervention on your behalf could you succeed. This represents an acceptance of God's sovereign power over all situations and circumstances. It is at this stage that the grace of God is released and the situation that at first looks indefatigable and insurmountable suddenly gives way and impossibility becomes possible. David trusted his God, the God Almighty and he was given the grace to overcome and defeat all his enemies.

Pastor Stephen Bawa has used this book to show how the power of the grace of God can be used to accomplish the above enumerated areas of a Christian life. The book is highly commended by its contents: the episodes and examples given, to teach the power of the grace of God to both new and old Christian believers.

Pastor Dr Samuel B, Goddy

July 10th, 2021

FORWARD BY REV DR JOHN CLEMENTS

For many years before I was called to pastor the oldest Congregational Church in the UK, I was engaged for a short time as an agony uncle on a London weekly newspaper. Each week the post Many brought countless letters from people who were at their wits end for one reason or another. The one thing they all had in common was the desire to find a better life. Back then as I read the sad stories of these people's lives, I constantly thanked God that by His grace I had been spared from many of these tragedies.

Sadly, it's a fact of life that bad things happen even in the lives of good people. The key is how we respond to these difficulties and challenges. Many can only see the negative and let themselves sink like lead balloons into spiralling depression. But there are some who by the grace of God not only overcome these setbacks but use them as steppingstones to better and more fulfilling lives.

I was therefore delighted some months ago to receive a request by Stephen Bawa to write this short forward to this little book that you are holding in your hands. He is a man who by God's grace has overcome many setbacks. In recent years he lost his wonderful wife Dorothy and has dedicated this book to her memory. He begins this book by sharing a powerful testimony of how out of the blue, one day he turned up for work and without any warning was dismissed that very day. Things like this destroy many people but in a remarkable way by God's grace he has overcome that setback.

According to Wikipedia in 2018 there were 188,000 books published in the UK. To read them all would take a lifetime, but can I urge you to find the time to read this book which I am sure you can read in about two to three hours. I am very selective in what I read these days as there are so many authors seeking your attention and sadly have very little to say of any real value. Worse still many are promoting theories that have no solid foundation and rather than help you will lead you astray. I have had the privilege of meeting Stephen Bawa and I can testify that he is one of the most authentic Christian men that I have met during last 73 years of my life! What he shares is based on eternal truth.

I know that as you turn the pages of this book you will encounter life changing truth. You will find answers to many of your questions about life and perhaps make the greatest discovery of your life that there is a God who loves and cares for you. I hope you will come to treasure this life changing book as much as I do.

May I wish you God's speed in your quest for a better life.

Dr Rev John Clements

Pastor, Old Meeting House Congregational Church,

Norwich, England.

INTRODUCTION

The concise Oxford Dictionary describes grace as the unmerited favour of God and a divine saving and strengthening influence. It further says that grace is an attractive feature. Most people whether they are Christians or not will agree with these two definitions. Grace is indeed an unmerited favour which means it is rare and not universally available to all. It also means because of its rarity; the recipients of grace are immensely privileged.

As a religious concept grace is exclusive to Christianity both in terms of its teaching contents as subject matter and in its application in practical Christianity. Grace is a unique theological concept that when properly understood and correctly applied confers boldness and supernatural confidence on its beneficiaries. Grace is not the same as faith; it is fundamentally different in its functions in that it brings the biblical Christian faith to perfection

(2 Corinthians 12:9). While faith is a set of beliefs in the fundamentals of religious creeds and theology; grace through the impartation of the Holy Spirit provides the enabling power and authority a believer needs to navigate the difficult and dangerous path of Christian life.

If it is impossible to please God without faith, it is doubly impossible to live a biblical Christian life without grace, let alone to please Him. Grace is audacious and emboldening, by grace a most wretched sinner is granted the audacity to stand before the most holy and awesome God and be called the son or daughter of the Almighty God. Grace produces good standing; makes intimacy with God possible and confers God's pure holiness on the notorious, wretched, and undeserving sinners.

This book reiterates the audacity of grace which enables man to build and sustains intimate relationship between the great and awesome God of all creation and puny wholly insignificant man. Grace then is the biggest miracle of all created by God entirely out of undeserving mercy for the benefit of humanity. Grace takes for granted the notion of personal unworthiness; it ignores critical and legalistic mind set and rejects outright the self-serving and arrogant work orientation as pre-requisite for winning God's favour here on the earth and in heaven hereafter. Grace insists that the salvation of God is available and given free of charge only by Jesus Christ the Saviour and the Redeemer of the mankind through the work He personally did on the Cross by shedding His precious blood as the supreme sacrifice for the redemption of sinners.

Stephen Bawa

The Kingdom Ministries

London, England

June, 2021

CHAPTER 1
MY GRACE IS SUFFICIENT FOR YOU
2 CORINTHIANS 12: 9

The morning had started with an ominous sign of impending despair; the weather was uncompromisingly dull when fresh wintry drips suddenly gave way as the sky turned into deep grey. I watched with increasing concern as the gentle drips changed into heavy drenching rain. I peered through the windscreen as I drove to work in the driving rain and midst of heavy London's morning traffic which was held up. I was hoping to catch a sign to assure me the weather conditions were improving but alas it was not.

I managed to get to the office somehow and parked my car at my allotted parking space and walked hurriedly to my office which was ten minutes away. I arrived at my desk drenched and cold, my umbrella having been blown away, as I walked from the parking bay by an unusually strong easterly wind.

At last, I finally arrived at work and made straight for my office. Some thirty minutes later I was informed by my secretary that the Chairman had unexpectedly announced that he was on his way to see me; this was something I had not expected as my diary was already full.

Nevertheless, I told my secretary to invite him into my office.

"I am not here for a social call I am afraid" said John politely but firmly. He then went on to explain that he had come to the regrettable conclusion that he could not work with me and therefore, he had come to inform me that my contract as the Managing Director with the Company was to be terminated forthwith. He further informed me that he had convened an Emergency Board meeting later in the afternoon at which he would report my departure. At the end of this conversation, he demanded that I hand over to him the keys to my office. For some strange reason which I could not explain, I did not say a word, neither did I attempt to stand my ground – normally being someone who never suffered fools gladly, I would have taken John to task, demanded to know on what grounds he had come to such a conclusion given the record of my achievements with the company within such a relatively short period of time. Instead, quite unbelievably I just simply reached for my briefcase and handed over the keys to him as requested. John ever the gentleman, offered to see me through the door; he then shook my hand very warmly and I was led out into the cold raining winter day.

By the time I got back to my car, my dripping wet clothes and sorry state reflected the condition of my inner being – sad, dejected and utterly defeated; I crumbled inside the car and attempted to drive. To my surprise having kick started the engine I found I was unable to drive.

I sat for hours at the wheel unable to make any sense of what had just happened so unexpectedly. I searched in vain within myself for some rational explanations or mistakes that I had overlooked, things that I could have done that I should have done better; things that I had done which I should not have done or done very differently. Unable to find any comforting answers; I finally I broke down before the Lord.

To back track and to put you into the picture, four months earlier I had taken up the job as Managing Director after having come out as the finest candidate following four marathon interviews and lengthy presentations to the whole Board of Directors. Throughout the interview process, John did not bother to disguise the fact that I was not his favourite candidate for the job. But as he was the only one in a Panel of five members who disapproved of me, he was consistently outvoted at every stage by four to one.

Having been given this information when I commenced, I had made sure that I put a double effort into my work. I put in a considerable amount of overtime in at the office, sometimes working till very late at night and even working into the week ends – in an effort to justify the vote of confidence shown in me given by the

Appointment Board. My efforts had paid off; I restructured the organisation's entire administrative and financial management systems much to the satisfaction and approval of the Board, funders, and stakeholders alike. A new training program was initiated for my Senior Management Team and the whole administration and financial management system was streamlined and computerised. Furthermore, a new Strategic and Development Plan was drawn up and presented to the Board of Directors for approval and this Plan was approved with commendation from the whole Board. I had succeeded even beyond my own expectation in my fund-raising strategy – resulting in doubling the funds raised and securing new partners and funders for the charity. Furthermore, I had carried out a thorough restructuring of the Company's information systems and got rid of the outdated and antiquated computers and had them replaced by new ones.

I had taken on this position almost as a vocation – I wanted to do my utmost for the Charity's beneficiaries by helping to develop and expand the services the organisation provided. I was very happy with my achievements within such a short space of time and had no indication of this calamity coming at all. This explains why I felt totally numbed and speechless when the chairman broke his bad news.

Now aged nearly fifty and finding myself unexpectedly unemployed – I suddenly felt a sense of total failure. I had a wife, a teenage son to support and a large monthly mortgage payment to service. A prolonged period of nonpayment of this mortgage would almost certainly result in the repossession of the family home. I had hoped to achieve something for the Lord in this new job by adopting a Christian vocational attitude to every task that I undertook in the position. Now that this managerial position had been unceremoniously brought to an untimely end I felt I had let the Lord down. It was at this time that the Lord spoke to me, not audibly through my ears, but directly through my heart. The essence of the word was divided into three parts:

1. Every true Christian ministry has an equal worth and value to the Lord.
2. Every true talent and blessing are given directly by God.
3. No one receives anything from God except through free grace.

At first, I was startled by these words because the first sentence was at variance with my unspoken and unconscious theology. I am a great believer in power evangelism – I am always in awe of those who are blessed with the capacity for miracles and wonders. To see the Lord, move in power through major miracles of healing the sick; raising the dead, delivering people from satanic oppression etc. always made my day. I rejoiced greatly whenever I saw or heard of these demonstrations of the Lord's power anywhere in the world. I therefore tended to see this display of power as belonging to the giants of the Christian faith as compared with those who only lived a mundane, pitiful and ordinary Christian life. Sadly, my daily experience had only been with the pigmies of the faith, but I longed for more.

This belief has led me to compare myself as well as other Christians that are not so blessed with this extra-ordinary ministry as minor Christians – not part of the elite circle of God's servants. To me therefore to infer that the likes of Benny Hinn, Reinhardt Bonke and Pastor Enoch Adeboye of the Redeemed Christian Church of God are of the same standing and of equal worth compared to insignificant and unprofitable Christians like me was an unacceptable arrogance. It is like saying that major Christian leaders like St. Paul, a five-star General in the Kingdom and I, a mere unprofitable, unreliable, and weak foot soldier – are of equal worth in the Kingdom – clearly an unreasonable proposition. But this teaching is nowhere to be found in the Bible as we are all equal in the sight of God.

> *"Every true ministry has equal value to God"*

It took me sometime to come to terms with this word of the Lord. First, the word `valid` is loaded and capable of double meaning: for there to be a `valid`, there must correspondingly be an `invalid`. I was more puzzled by this thought because, can an ordained ministry be ever described as `invalid`? I was told that a ministry could start at first as a valid ministry but later become invalid because such a ministry has stopped being God focused – regardless as to how such ministry came into being and is currently perceived by the body of Christ and the world.

The one that remains Christ centred to the end is the one that is valid. All valid ministries serve the purposes of God in each generation. God's approval is the only deciding factor and that genuine obedience to the leading of the Spirit of God is the key.

The Lord helped me to understand that my notion of what was important, and worthy was not the same as His notion. If it is the desire of the Lord that a man's ministry is to wash dishes in Old People's Home; he will be equipped with the Spirit of the Lord to achieve the purpose of this task to the glory of God. You might have come across the wonderful story of a humble monk called Brother Lawrence, who worked in the soup kitchen of his monastery, he wrote the amazing book, "The Practice of the Presence of God". If he persists to the end doing this lowly task with all his heart, he will be rewarded on the day of glory with the reward of equal value to that given to Saint Paul, Elijah, and Moses.

I was told further that however if the same minister, for all Christians are God's ministers; were to conclude that he would rather be a tele-evangelist and start performing wonders and miracles in the name of the Lord; his newly found ministry may be very successful in the eyes of the world and even in the eyes of the body of Christ. He will however receive no reward from the Lord on the day of glory because God is not obligated to bless in eternity that which He had not commanded, nor will He ever reward disobedience under any circumstance. God is no respecter of persons!

The case in point here is that of King Saul, who was told to go and wage war against the known enemies of God. He was specifically told not to take any spoil of war; his clear instructions were to utterly wipe out everything in sight. King Saul only partially obeyed the order, he went to war and was successful in defeating the enemies but kept the cattle alive as spoil of war. King Saul was told that his disobedience was tantamount to idolatry and subsequently God rejected him as King over Israel, and he was replaced by King David. (1 Sam 13:1 to 15:33)

I was later to learn the importance of this fact when I was subsequently drawn to the word of Paul to the new Christians in Corinthian where he said that he had by grace laid the foundation as a wise builder. This foundation he went on to explain was Christ – he then warns individual Christians who are going to build on the foundation to watch out for what they are building on this foundation because on the day of judgement when we would all appear in front of the throne of Christ to receive our reward for our efforts for what we have done here on earth. In order to determine our reward, the intrinsic quality of our work will be tested with fire. This fire of God will reveal the true nature of our contribution based on God's impartial and exceedingly just criteria (1 Corinthians 3: 10 – 15).

There are apparently two kinds of Judgement seats of God: the first one is the judgement seat of condemnation where the sins of the individual non-Christian believers will be judged and have a sentence of eternal damnation pronounced. It is a Judgment seat of condemnation precisely because everyone arraigned to appear before it has already been judged by their own sins mainly because they failed to accept the mercy and grace of God made available by the Lord Jesus Christ the only Saviour and Redeemer of the mankind; the purpose of appearing before this gruesome seat is to receive the verdict in person: God does not judge anyone, and the proceedings in front of the seat is very much unlike the Court proceedings here on earth with the Prosecution and the Defence Teams arguing for and against the charges; there would be no technical or finer points of law to contend with and no circumstantial evidence that could be subject to differing interpretations. God's inviolate standard of justice would be the only criteria for reaching judgment which would be irrevocably final and not subject to appeal.

What is more the verdict would be incontrovertible as the evidence would be clear for all to see: the wages of sin is eternal death, an eternal separation from God (Romans 6: 23) and because all have sinned and come short of the glory of glory of God (Romans 3: 23).

Christians who have been washed by the blood and the righteousness of Jesus Christ the Saviour and the Redeemer of the Mankind will not appear before this Seat of Judgement because they have passed from the Judgement of death into life: their sins having been washed by the Blood of the Lamb of God.

The second Seat is the Seat of Rewards. This is where Christians will be assembled, and each will appear before the Throne of God to receive rewards for what they had done in the flesh here on earth. Again, here there is no controversy either. The Book of life would be opened, and the individual names called out to appear before God. Each person's work would be revealed against the quality standard of heaven.

The fire of God will reveal some work to be of superior quality in the form of gold, sapphire, and ruby whilst some others will be found to be no more than rubble. The rubbishy work will not survive the fire test and its owner will receive nothing for their effort from the Lord. We will return to this crucial matter and brutal fact later in the book.

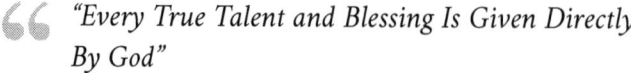

"Every True Talent and Blessing Is Given Directly By God"

The Spirit of the Lord made it clear to me very vividly that all genuine talents, valid ministry, and every blessing comes directly from God the Father notwithstanding whether these talents and blessings are used correctly as God intended or misused to serve the interest of the flesh and evil purposes.

The meaning of this word in the circumstances and the predicament I was in at the time startled me. Am I to understand that although I had done all I could possibly do to impress my employer by adopting a Christian attitude to work and by working tirelessly; and despite all these, the man who unjustly fired me, did so by using the position and the talents my God had given him? How could God allow the gift He had given to be so misused to perpetrate such a callous injustice against His son – i.e., myself?

It was at this juncture that I reminded myself of the commitment I had previously undertaken to the effect that no matter how strange any move of God might appear to me, my reaction to the given situation must invariably be to adopt the attitude of trust in the essential goodness of the Lord and the willingness to obey His spirit leading unquestionably in spite of - or regardless of my ignorance and lack of understanding of His ultimate plan. It is enough for me to know that my God could invariably be relied upon regardless to do the very best for me in all circumstances of life.

I arrived home completely exhausted and totally dejected. I immediately headed straight to my small prayer room intending to confront God and calling down the Elijah fire on the perpetrator of my predicament. But for some strange reason as I started praying, my rage against the outrage that had just been perpetrated had subsided somewhat as I had no energy left to fight any battle with man let alone with God! Instead, I found myself praying incoherently and mumbling with trepidation seeking to find out from the Lord what would be the way forward for me and my family in the midst of this devastation. The more I prayed the weaker I got until finally I gave up the effort because I was not receiving any answer or feed back from the Lord.

Then suddenly I seemed to remember at last the word of the Lord which says, 'My grace is sufficient for you' (2 Corinthians 12: 9). I immediately pounced on this word as I realized that this was the same word said to St. Paul by the Lord in answer to his petition when he was going through his own trials and tribulations.

> "No one receives anything except through my free grace."

In the scripture quoted above, Paul was told by God that His grace given to him was more than sufficient to see Paul though his weaknesses and ordeal and to make him triumphant despite many obstacles and suffering that he was going through at the time. This is what Paul said in relation to the word God spoke to him: 'Most gladly therefore will I rather glory in my infirmities that the power of Christ may rest upon me. Therefore, I take pleasure in infirmities, in reproaches, in necessities, in persecutions, in distresses for Christ's sake: for when I am weak, then am I strong' (2 Corinthians 12:9–10). However, grace does more than that: all abilities, competencies and blessings are directly given by God without reference to any meritocratic qualifications.

We see the evidence of this plainly in God's word: "who has first given Me anything so that I could recompense – has my Hand not created all things?" (Job 41: 11).

I later came to understand that nobody can impress God, nor can anyone make justified demands on Him on the basis of merit. A person endued with talents and skills in whatever areas of human endeavour has not been so favoured because he has done something quite extraordinary that made him deserve such favour – he has received these gifts purely by the free grace of God. What is true of the skills and competencies in the physical realm is also true of the spiritual realm. Indeed, the greatest gift of all, the gift of salvation through Christ's atonement was based on the pure grace of God.

The Holy Spirit was able to impress the truth of God's word regarding the concept of free grace on my mind and this enabled me to get over the shock of what I considered to be an unmitigated calamity. With the sudden realisation that if the grace of God was sufficient for Paul and the records show that Paul went on in spite of the plethora of obstacles put his way to become the Prince and the most successful Apostle of his age and indeed of any age; then there is no reason why I should not overcome the seemingly insurmountable problem I was confronted with.

And what became of my heartfelt prayer and outcry to God against the apparent injustice and unfairness perpetrated against me by John, the Chairman?

The Lord did not give me permission to appeal to the Board to reverse John's unfair and unjust action. Instead, the Lord showed me the whole organisation would soon be no more. I saw in my dream the whole building went into what looked like a premature decay, completely derelict, dilapidated and covered in cobwebs. At the time, I did not understand how a brand-new modern Office building could undergo a very rapid decay, literally withered, and abandoned even though the office building was located in the fashionable part of London business district.

It was some fifteen years later when I had completely recovered and had totally forgotten the sad experience that I was told what became of the Company. One of the Senior Executives on my Management Team saw me at a Management Seminar and hesitatingly approached me. He introduced himself and apologised for interrupting my Coffee break. He then proceeded to tell me what happened on the day of my departure when I was unceremoniously dismissed as the Managing Director.

No one had any knowledge of what had transpired as the Chairman did not tell my Management Team of my dismissal for fear, he would be confronted to explain his action. My absence only became noticeable when I failed to turn up at the Board meeting the following day. It was then that the pandemonium broke out and the Chairman was taken to task for his illegal action which was clearly seen to have been motivated by blatant racism and discrimination.

Within a month the whole organisation was in turmoil and within two months after my departure, the entire Board was sacked, and the Company closed as each of the stakeholders and funders withdrew their support one after the other. As he narrated the story, I busted into tears as I was overwhelmed by the love and care of God our Father. The extent that He would go to fight the battles of His children who may at first seem powerless to fight for themselves against seemingly powerful and well-established enemy. I learnt a very important lesson on that day, that our Father is a God of absolute integrity; that He would keep to His word to fight against the enemies of His children. To God our Father be glory, honour, praise, and power for all eternity – Amen!

Did I recover from this great setback?

Yes, indeed I did as the Father God opened a new door that I did not know was literally waiting for me. The Lord spoke through emphatic prophetic utterances from one of His Canadian servants of God at a Christian Conference held in London. The man who never knew me or had met me before delivered a message from the Lord and directed me twice in the same day ordering me to step up a company using the skills and competencies, He had invested in me.

Following these direct instructions from the Lord; I set up a Consulting Firm specialising in Management Consultancy and Training. The favour of God and His grace was very much evident in the Company because everything I needed including modern spacious office building, computers, office furniture and fittings were provided by God through a miraculous and divine intervention. I was given the Headquarters Office of a successful Construction firm who had decided to relocate to larger premises leaving behind a beautifully designed office accommodation with brand new carpets, excellent heating system and well-connected ultra-modern ICT cables and expensive modern telecommunication equipment. The Lord gave me His favour with the Landlord of the premises who apparently for no reason at all decided to give me a one-year rent holiday and without me asking him for it. I was also blessed by the Lord through a friend who was a Senior Executive of a well-known Insurance Company. His Company was relocating the Regional Headquarters to Bournemouth, and he was willing to give me all their newly acquired Computers and including very expensive Executive furniture. When I added together the value of the various presents including the one-year rent holiday that the Father God had given me, it came very close to some £100,000. For a penniless executive looking to restart his fractured career, this was an unbelievable turnaround of fortune and an unexpected mercy of God. The Father God also provided finances which enabled us to hire the services of the highly qualified Computer Engineers and various highly trained Management experts to come work for me. Our God is a wonderful God, way maker and an ardent promise keeper and Light in the darkness.

Within two years of my unjust dismissal a very successful company employing over 50 staff and four Directors with five branches in the English regions and running over £10 million contract for the British Government came into being – and all of these were made possible only by the grace of God.

CHAPTER 2
THE AUDACITY OF GRACE

> "But Noah found grace with God"
>
> — GENESIS 6 VS 8

What is grace? There are many words connected and related to grace – there is 'grace' as in, 'graceful' and 'gracious'. We will consider many definitions of grace in this chapter. Some people have described grace as an 'unmerited favour' – that is a favour that is given without the recipient having any expectation or entitlement to the favour bestowed on them or having done nothing whatsoever to deserve it.

Others see grace as a higher form of mercy – mercy is receiving an undeserved favour this usually applies in a judicial environment of criminal justice system when an accused person stands condemned on the strength of valid available and reliable evidence in a court of capable jurisdiction. However, the Judge using his discretionary power then decides to use his prerogative to show mercy in the dispensation of justice by either letting the accused go free or passing a sentence that carries with it the barest minimum of conviction. This is called 'tempering justice with mercy'. The accused is guilty and is found guilty under the law, but the full weight and the rigour of law – the normal consequences that should follow the breaking of a criminal code is not applied and the guilty man is allowed to go free.

Mercy and grace have many characteristics in common, but the two concepts are intrinsically different. They are both premised on the fact that: the beneficiaries have not worked in order to receive what they are given and there is no sense of entitlement. Secondly, there is no principle of strict merit at play, the notion of fairness in the ordinary use of the word is invariably seriously tempered. The basis of an ordinary objective fairness is that a plain field exists where action is directly correlated to the results achieved in an egalitarian non-partial environment under known and accepted conditions operating under a universally recognized framework. Not only is there no partiality, but there is no favouritism either and the whole regime is conducted under a truly observable transparency and objectivity. Fairness and justice emphasise an unadulterated and rigid compliance with the rules, terms, and conditions within given boundaries. The rules of the game are known to all participants and the compliance with the regulations are applied uniformly, blindly, and regimentally. However, the introduction of the concept of favour and grace inevitably undermines the strict interpretation of fairness and justice when a man is allowed to receive that which he does not deserve and that for which he has not worked. This remains the case irrespective of whether the act of kindness or mercy is applied under positive or negative dispensation.

Grace carries with it so many different meanings and interpretations. Being 'graceful' for example – to be graceful or be seeing to be graceful is either to act or behave in graceful manners with pleasant and amiable personality or to be in possession of some unusual talents either with physical dexterity or being in possession of some unusual prowess that is deemed socially highly valued and economically useful. An accomplished and talented ballet dancer who dances beautifully and delightfully is commended for moving gracefully through the dance movements effortlessly without regard and with no apparent signs of pain in spite of technical difficulty involved in the dance routines.

A person is said to have acted gracefully because they have behaved commendably beyond the normal expectation under the given circumstances – where they might have been jolly well excused had they behaved less charitably. To be graceful is to go beyond the call of duty – to go an extra mile and to act and behave better than the current situation objectively warrants or demands.

Similarly, to be gracious – an extension of being 'graceful' is to show magnanimity in the face of provocation and unfair trial. A person is said to be gracious when they display an unusual kind of gentleness, kindness and understanding in each testing situation to an undeserving person or in circumstances where the display of such virtues is not generally expected.

There are many notions or forms of grace. In commercial transactions involving loans and mortgages, the terms and conditions of trade usually stipulate a time during which the borrower will not be required to make any instalment payment - this is called a 'period of grace'. This is a temporary respite before the repayment of the loans fully commences. In some circumstances, the borrower could during this 'period of grace' change their mind about the whole transaction and back out of the deal altogether. If this is done during the 'period of grace' the borrower will not incur any financial penalty. However, this favourable condition elapses automatically and no longer operates as soon as the 'period of grace' expires.

A major difference between grace and mercy is that mercy is a free and unfettered exercise of the sovereign will of the benefactor, the recipient of mercy has no entitlement that is either legally or morally enforceable. No matter how many times the deeds of mercy have been dispensed, the beneficiaries cannot rely on its ceaseless continuity in perpetuity – mercy can be discontinued, suspended or terminated at any time of the benefactor's choosing. Mercy therefore is not permanent and it is usually exercised on given situations mostly of past events. Grace on the other hand is dependent on a priori action of a benefactor expressly undertaken intentionally and stored up for the exclusive benefit of the intended beneficiaries, with legal underpinnings that convey legitimacy – grace is enabling on continuous basis both on the present and future use. The grace once it is given is available for use by the recipient immediately and for ever or at least for the duration of the lifetime of the beneficiary. Grace confers entitlement on the beneficiary position, privileges, abilities and rights from which ordinarily the beneficiary would otherwise have been legitimately precluded.

In Genesis chapter 6, verse 8, we find that God was very gracious to Noah and his household. The situation in the days of Noah had become dire – godlessness has reached an unacceptable level of unbelievable savagery.

"And God saw that the wickedness of man was great in the earth, and that every imagination of the thoughts of his heart was only evil continually. And it repented the Lord that He had made man on the earth, and it grieved Him at His heart." (Gen. 6:5– 7).

In verse 8 of the same chapter, it says: "But Noah found grace in the eyes of the Lord. This means Noah did not do anything at all for God in order to receive this grace. If this had not been so, we would have been told what deed of piety and greatness Noah had done. We see similar unconditional sovereign act of love and mercy demonstrated by God the Father when Jesus Christ the Saviour and the Redeemer of the mankind announced His Father's love for humanity in the book of John chapter 3, verse 16 'For God so love the world that He gave His only begotten Son. The Lord Jesus Christ did not give us any reason why it was that His Father just happened to so love the world! The love that the Father had for the world was certainly not obtained as the result of what the world had done to deserve the love, on the contrary, the world had done grievous evil before the Lord and the love was as a result of what the Father had initiated Himself because of who He is and His love.

Later on, in verses 9 to 11, we are given the genealogy of Noah and at verse 9, we have this said of Noah: "Noah was a just man and perfect in his generations and Noah walked with God." We know that it could never be said that Noah was saintly and that he had no sin at all; because the Bible says all have sinned and come short of the glory of God (Romans 3: 23). The Bible is insistent about the culpability of all souls before God – including that of Noah. The verdict is abundantly clear about human susceptibility to the stain of sin; all sons and daughters of Adam are guilty before God and none including Noah is excluded, no, not one.

How come then that Noah received such a glowing character reference and commendation from the Almighty God in relation to Noah's integrity, perfection, and holiness – especially in the face of the uncompromising declaration of the holy writ? The answer is very clear: 'Noah found grace with God'. There has been suggestions that Noah's acceptance by God was due largely to the fact that his assumed perfection was not due to his spiritual holiness but essentially due to his genealogical pedigree and undiluted genetic make up. The days of Noah were dominated by the hybrid race of man-demon giants called the Nephilims. The so called sons of God (Demons the fallen angels driven by God out of heaven with Satan) had by that time polluted the gene pool of humanity by literally and physically taken over the body of men of the age and through the seducing spirit and had had sexual intercourse with human females. This union had produced in very large numbers giant offsprings with rebellious, sinful and wicked characteristics that were totally unacceptable to God (Genesis 6: 2 - 4). Thank goodness Noah and his immediate family did not originate from the corruption of this satanic experiment. Although the Bible does not expressly state this fact, but it is reasonable to assume that the subsequent destruction by flood of the Noah's generation was due largely to the wickedness, extreme perversion and utterly demonic godlessness instigated by Satan and the Nephilims. The scriptures may have been referring to Noah's unadulterated human genealogical heritage rather than his moral and spiritual perfection.

What the Bible is clear about is that the grace that Noah had conferred on him absolved him entirely from all his sins because having secured the favour of God he has been justified freely and redeemed. To understand this better you need to know that our God operates in the realm of eternity outside of the human time framework. Put it simply the Mighty One who tells the outcomes of the end right from the beginning had looked across the centuries of the future not yet in being and had allowed by sovereign act of mercy, His grace through Jesus's blood 'whom God had set forth to be propitiation through faith in His blood, to declare His righteousness for the remission of Noah's sins through the forbearance of God' (Romans 3: 25).

Noah's steadfast walk with God in the eyes of grace has qualified him by faith to have him justified, thoroughly washed by the blood of the Lamb of God – and all without the deeds of the law – wow! (Romans 3: 28) But that is not all; the Almighty God further conferred the gift of sanctification on Noah to make him become the righteousness of God – an immaculate being entirely without sin, stains, or wrinkles. In other words, Noah was made a perfect man through the righteousness of God. Here unmistakably in our very eyes is the unbelievable demonstration of the audacity of grace.

Why was Noah so different from other men of his evil generation? Why was it that Noah alone was reported to have been perfect and seemingly set apart even from his friends and family? There was no lengthy explanation about how Noah came to be so radically different from the people and the prevailing evil culture around him – we are not even given any example of his good deeds, his generosity of spirit, his kindness to his neighbours or how much he cared about nature or how much he loved his wife and children. Furthermore, although we are told he walked with God, but just how he managed to do that whilst everybody else became satanic, we are not told, neither are we told what his walk with God actually entailed.

This is because the Almighty God is the final arbiter, the ultimate decider, and the final sole judge of what is righteous and holy. God is not concerned about what people's opinions of Noah were neither was He concerned about the need to parade His servant's good deeds in order to secure the approval of men. Noah's good deeds and righteousness consist mainly in God alone.

In the book of Psalms Chapter 32 the Bible says in verses 1 and 2 "blessed is the man to whom the Lord does not impute sin" "Blessed is the man whose iniquities have been blotted out". In the New Testament Book of Hebrews Chapter 11, Apostle Paul says that Abraham believed in God and his faith was counted to him as righteousness. Here lies the secret of Noah's holiness. Noah like Abraham after him, believed in God and walked in obedience with Him. In return, the Almighty God counted Noah's and Abraham's faith as righteousness and blotted out their sins by grace – praise God!

Friends, the Lord of the Noah's day is exactly the same God of our days because He does not change (Malachi 3:5). His love for you is not dependent on the opinions held by other people about you and even more surprisingly, neither does it depend on your own assumptions about yourself – His perception of you is entirely motivated by and dependent on His love for you. It is good to maintain good relations with all men because our Lord Jesus Christ commanded us to be at peace with all men. However, the most important relationship that will stand the test of time is the relationship we cultivate and maintain with our Father God. That this is the case provides an enormous relief for which God must be praised for ever. Human perceptions are notoriously unreliable, and our opinions are heavily influenced by the prejudices acquired through long experience and cultural socialization much of which is radically at variance with basic biblical Christianity.

Friend do not be unduly influenced by the opinions of man – except in so far as they are in conformity with the word of God; even then make doubly sure that the context is accurate, and the interpretation is as given in the Scriptures.

Humans judge by what they see and hear or what they think they see through the tainted and inexact spectacles of cultural relativity; the ever changing and shifting conventional wisdom of the age. This is the reason why Christians must stop seeking the approval of men or strive to conform to the prevailing worldview of a dubious progressive ideology. Thanks be to God that our Lord and His standard of justice and holiness remain immutable and His love unchanging for all eternity. The secret of joy in the Lord is the sure knowledge that He is the rewarder of those who diligently seek Him and then to build our faith and action on this salient truth of seeking God with all our heart, mind, body and soul.

Our God is a God of absolute integrity, and He is utterly dependable. He has an impeccable record of forever keeping to His word 'I will be diligent to keep to my word says the Lord. My word will not return to me void, but it will achieve the purpose for which I sent it – (Isaiah 55: 11)

On closer examination, we find that Noah's secret lies in verse 8 of the chapter: "But Noah found grace in the eyes of the Lord". Apparently, it was the grace that Noah found with the Lord that set him apart from everybody else. And it shows, it was only after he found grace that we are told that he became perfect. It is clear then that the basis of Noah's moral superiority and character perfection consists mainly of the grace he received from God and nothing else – wow!

This is the classic nature of grace: grace justifies, it sets apart, and it empowers. Grace enriches; enlarges and impacts creativity as well as multiplies blessings and blessedness exponentially.

Noah was justified by the grace which was initiated by God. This grace enabled Noah to walk in faith with the Lord and as we have found in Abraham, his faith was counted unto him as righteousness. The good standing which Noah had obtained from God led to him being justified to the point that whatever Noah might have done wrong in the past was no longer imputed to him – henceforth God was only interested in dealing with Noah on the basis of grace, and now Noah was covered by the very righteousness of God Himself.

The justification received by Noah under grace now set him apart and made him qualified for salvation, it also made him qualified to be appointed as God's partner in the subsequent work of global cleansing and redemption.

Noah was drafted into the secret plans of the Most High God and was given the blueprint of God's rescue plan for humanity.

Here before us we see a clear evidence of the audacity of grace. Noah - a mere mortal living among the worst possible criminals and sinners of his days; deeply soaked in a culture of utter depravity in a totally godless age was given an unbelievable privilege of being a God's confidant.

No one else on the earth knew the intended plan of God except Noah. What is more and here is the extraordinarily unthinkable proposition – neither was anyone in heaven outside of the Godhead. That this took place is beyond doubt. The Bible is very clear about this matter – the Almighty Himself conducted all the negotiations with Noah directly without using angelic intermediaries. God did not send a single Angel as messenger to convey His plan to Noah – not even an Archangel. Under the dispensation of grace, a close and intense personal relationship between the Almighty God and man is possible. Grace turned Noah an ordinary mortal to an extraordinary man of great importance the world has ever seen. The first faithful servant of global proportions with eternal relevance!

It is possible you may have thought of yourself as a person of no importance – an inconsequential man or woman of little relevance. Maybe you have been told so often that you would not amount to anything in life and sure enough, you yourself have come to believe these lies.

Perhaps indeed, you find yourself – alone on your own. Not so if you are a child of the Almighty God. You may be as small as a Lilliputian, but with a little touch from God of grace and immediately you are transformed by His grace to the most powerful giant that has ever lived.

Listen the child of God; nothing is too difficult for your Father. Watch and marvel at the doings of this incredible God who turned a strong and powerful battled hardened giant and General called Goliath into a helpless and confused lump in the middle of an existential battle with an inexperienced skinny teenager called David. Grace caused the fearsome warrior that had become a terror to the entire Army of Israel to meet his waterloo at the hand of a child. With his destruction, the honour of an horrified and discredited nation was restored, and God was glorified. You see grace restores the lost honours, glory and wasted opportunities.

But it does not stop there, because grace does more, much more – grace enables. It provides supra-abundant ability, capability, and strength to its beneficiaries. A man in possession of the grace of God can do all things effortlessly. Whilst everyman and woman of Noah's days were steeped in sin and godlessness, the Holy Spirit bears witness to Noah's moral uprightness and implacable integrity. How did he achieve this commendable life of holiness whilst living in the environment of the overwhelming cesspit of sin? The answer is grace!

Maybe you are struggling to live a Christian life and it would appear the more you try the more you seem to fail. As you force yourself to take one step forward, you are immediately assailed by an onslaught that seem to compel you to go two steps backwards - thus making a breakthrough over sin an impossible dream for you. You have written yourself off because of the obvious weaknesses and imperfections that you believe are deeply ingrained in your personality. I have good news for you. I would recommend the grace of God to you.

It may well be that you are very prayerful, and a person of strong faith and you have been seeking the Lord with very little evidence of success to your credit. Now the tiredness is settling in and with doubts – crippling doubts that are beginning to eat deep into the fabric and foundation of your faith in Christ. The passion you once had when you first heard the good news of the kingdom and the enthusiasm you had shown when you first received Christ as your Lord and Saviour is steadily ebbing away and consequently your joy in your Lord is producing diminishing returns. Friend, I plead with you to flee to God of grace and rest.

It may be that the hope and aspiration you once had of serving the Lord with all your heart is gradually fading because the promises and prophecies given to you are taking a little bit longer to come to pass and this delayed expectation is causing you to lose heart. Child of God, delay is no deniance and your Father is still the same and His love for you will never fail. Although our Father does not move before His own appointed time – nevertheless, He never ever comes late, never!

The grace of God empowers us by the Holy Spirit of Christ to do the will of God and to flourish effortlessly in godly living regardless of the circumstances prevailing around us. Lot lived in Sodom and Gomorrah – the twin cities of sin with a record of blameless life in the midst of confusion and supercharged sexual and homosexual debauchery of his days. Lot was able to do this because of the power of God's grace that was at work in his life (Ephesians 3:20). We have promises of God given to us to invoke the ability and power to live a successful Christian and God honouring life by grace.

I beseech you to seek a fresh acquaintance with the grace of God and you will discover that your Father is ever so faithful and there is nothing that He would deny His children. The longer we wait to receive the promise, the more we will realise when the promise is finally delivered that it has been worth waiting for. Grace does impart patience and we learn obedience through patience. What is more, the quality of our commitment and integrity is tested through patience just as the quality of gold is enhanced by the length of time it is put through a purifying furnace.

Jacob served seven years twice for the love of Rachel and discovered that Rachel was worth waiting for after all. Moses waited for a solid forty years to fulfil his destiny after a tentative false start, and he was not disappointed. Joseph found that his steadfast waiting on God's promises for his life for such a long time was not in vain. He obtained all that he was promised by the Almighty without exception and the name of Joseph is forever inscribed in gold amongst the God's generals in the hall of fame. Remember this, child of God, our blessed Lord, the author, and the finisher of our faith Himself spent thirty years to prepare for a ministry of three and half years – that is about ten years of preparation for every one year of ministry!

Pray and ask God to open your heart and eyes to see what He is doing in your life that you cannot see with your physical eyes and the grace to obey the will of God for your life. In the Paul's epistle to the Hebrews Chapter 4 the Holy Spirit invites us to: "come boldly to the throne of grace, that we may obtain mercy and grace to help us in time of need". These words make it categorically clear that God has appointed a way by which we can seek and obtain grace.

Please notice the invitation: you are invited not to the throne of holiness, or the throne of power, or the throne of judgment, or the throne of miracles. But you are invited to the throne of grace; why? This is because this is the only throne where you are a given the audacity to come boldly to obtain mercy and grace to help you in time of need. Are you in need of help? Do you find the Christian journey rather difficult to navigate? Are you struggling to discern the genuine will of God for your life at the moment?

Maybe you are at a crossroad of life: it has become a matter of now or never for you as you seek to serve the Lord and to heed His calling on your life. The years are rolling on and by and by and achieving your life destiny is becoming more and more distant as time changes and flies away beyond your reach whilst all your efforts at rescuing the situation have proven fruitless. You feel you are being left behind by forces over which you have little or no control? Then come to the throne of grace and reload. Come as you are without one plea, come to the God of Grace and come with boldness believing not in your own goodness but in the goodness of the Lord Jesus Christ alone.

The only way to receive the grace of God is by faith through persistent importunate prayer; bold and confident approach to the throne of grace, the most holy place of God's presence where our sympathising High Priest Jesus Christ the Saviour and the Redeemer of the Mankind has entered on our behalves, and He is waiting to hear us and grant our heartfelt requests – verses 14 – 15.

Let us now return to our story of Noah and the beauty of God's grace.

We see here that it was God Almighty Himself who initiated the deed of grace which Noah received, and his family subsequently benefited from. You may ask for mercy and plead for favour but the actual granting of any of these are outside of the influence and control you can muster – they are firmly and exclusively within the domain and personal prerogative of God the benefactor. This is the case unquestionably to all right-thinking people. You cannot contest your weak position and lack of entitlement; the Almighty is in no doubt of His full authority and prerogative to give or withhold favour without having to give account of His action to anyone.

The appointment of Noah was a deliberate choice taken by God alone to demonstrate His loving grace to the lost world. Grace imparts power, supernatural ability, creativity, innovations, skills and knowledge. No one had built a boat before because no one had the knowledge and skill set as well as tools required to build a boat that could withstand an avalanche and a deluge of great and raging body of heavy waters. Noah was not only chosen but he was also given a blueprint of the Boat he was to build and the detailed specifications, full instructions and training. Noah served an apprenticeship under the direction of the Holy Spirit on boat building craftsmanship. He was trained further on animal husbandry and given full instructions concerning the welfare of his family.

The lesson here is very clear. The Lord our God pays for what He orders! If He calls you to do anything for Him, He will most definitely provide all that is required to achieve His aim. God given vision always comes with a well prepared and fully resourced abundant provision in the long run. So, do not be afraid to step out of the boat or be discouraged because you could not possibly see how you would ever be able to finance the project God has put on your heart. Remember that if it is God's plan then He is obligated to provide all the resources needed to see the project through to the end very successfully.

We do not know the time span between the time the Lord called Noah to set up a boat yard and we do not know how long it took after He had downloaded the technical drawings and the exact specification software of the boat to be built unto Noah's brains. We do not for example know the number of years of apprenticeship training Noah must have undergone to become a qualified Master boat builder. What we do know is before any substantial project like the one Noah undertook could be accomplished, a considerable degree of planning would have been called for.

Without a doubt several different engineering skills and competencies would have been required as absolute prerequisites. That is not all, before you can contemplate building such a massive boat, you must first have to design and manufacture the various technical tools for different operations in the construction of the boat and these tools have to be produced in sufficient quantities and quality to the highest specification.

Furthermore, you will have to recruit and train the workforce to acquire the differing skills and competencies required to undertake the tasks of ship building and maintenance. Many of us who have had to lead and manage workforces of differing skills and competencies and different hierarchies know the complexity of large scale project management of this nature.

But for Noah, the situation was much harder because, no one had ever seen a boat before let alone built one – there was no prior experience to build on and no comparison which with to judge quality and carry out stress and durability test. But despite all these challenges, God made ways for Noah to accomplish his goals effortlessly and on record time. Child of God what was true of Noah is also true of you. Noah was led from the beginning to the end by God and the entire project was a resounding success from start to finish.

The plan was not Noah's plan, the objective was not Noah's objective and the project was not Noah's project – these were all conceived, planned and executed by God to perfection with super abundance supply of all provisions necessary to finish the task fully provided and on time.

The decision to wipe out the then humanity was taken by God, the calling of Noah and his immediate family was a singular act of God as well as the commissioning of the boat. God's absolute sovereignty is revealed in every aspect of Noah's action – indeed the whole story is not about Noah at all, but essentially about the God Almighty who meticulously planned and executed the plan with an absolutely accurate precision.

A further revelation of what is contained in the extra-ordinary story of Noah is the abundant display of the power of God over His creation. Have you ever considered the virtual impossibility of having lion and lioness cohabiting for forty days and forty nights with the lamb under the same roof without the lamb becoming an easy prey to the lions? How was it possible that the dangerous and highly poisonous reptiles like snakes and crocodiles could be restrained effectively for forty days and forty nights from attacking Noah and his family? This is even more surprising given the fact that there was no record of Noah and his family having access to any form of weaponry to defend themselves.

Why was there no pandemonium on the Boat given its assorted cargo? No breakout and no disturbance, no riot even though for forty nights and forty days these assortments of dangerous animals cohabited peacefully side by side in perfect brotherly love. Furthermore, the complex logistical planning that must have gone into the day to day running of the Boat, the administration of the massive feeding program and differing arrays of food stuff that must be provided and in sufficient quantities and water for all the dangerous passengers on the Boat for the duration of the journey.

Surely there must be more to this than meet the eye? Absolutely! Although Noah was superficially the Shepherd of the animals and the human residents of the Boat – but in reality, God Himself was absolutely in charge. There can be no danger where God is in charge. What proves impossible for man in the natural is no big deal at all for our God. Under the regime of the Almighty everything works perfectly together for good. The sovereign God has supreme power and authority over all His creation and at His command all things do His bidding.

Thus, a giant Whale became a submarine and a driverless transportation service for Prophet Jonah to convey him effortlessly to his destination in Nineveh. At the command of the Almighty God the hungry pride of Lions mysteriously became the bodyguards, giant kittens and playmates to Daniel the faithful servant of God - even though their expected role was to tear Daniel to pieces and have him for dinner!

Where our God is present, all perils disappear, and all dangers must flee. The same flame of powerful furnace which blew back and consumed the seven strong men who forcibly tossed the three children of God into the consuming fire in a matter of seconds because of its severity, suddenly turned to become a refuge and a bondage breaker for the three glorious servants of the Most High. Because God was in the fire, all that the fire was permitted to do was to remove the fetters and chains of His three faithful servants – their clothes, their shoes and the hair on their heads were preserved from being consumed by fire by the order of the Almighty. What is more, the Bible records, that there was no burning smell of fire or flame as the three men walked out of the terrible furnace. Even the fire itself had to obey its creator, the Almighty God.

There is a lot to learn from this that will benefit our own walk with God. No matter how seemingly difficult the task given to us by God may appears to be; and regardless of the presence of implacable obstructions and enemies, the grace of God will see us through to victory. For our God specialises in solving impossible problems. In the middle of the most intractable, discordant, and incongruous situation, the ingenuity of our God in providing solutions is beyond doubt.

In walking with God, your part of the bargain is strictly obedience, unshakeable faith that moves mountains. The Almighty God will ensure that the resources required as well as competences and capabilities to complete the task are made available in sufficient quantities and on time by the God for whom nothing, but nothing is impossible.

For us today, it is not very difficult to understand the need to build boats because we could see the need for it. The Bible does not indicate the exact geographical position of Noah's location or the Country and town in which Noah lived. For instance, we do not know whether Noah and his family lived in a coastal town where they were familiar with the power of the large body of waters and the seas. What we know is that at the time Noah was asked to build a boat, it had never rained on the earth before that time.

The idea of a deluge or tsunami that eventually led to a complete wipe out of all that was on the earth at the time must have been very strange and unheard of. There can be no doubt that Noah and his fellow ship builders must have been laughed at and treated as cranks and eccentrics at best and completely mad men at worst. There had never been a boat before, no one had ever seen one or known what a boat looked like. Secondly, a great deal of faith must have been needed to enable them to believe that something that had never happened before was going to happen – rain was going to fall. And not only that but that when the rain eventually came, it would come with such immense power and force that it would strip away everything on the face of the earth.

Furthermore, no one had ever built a boat before in the days of Noah because not only was there no need for it, but there was no knowledge or skills required to undertake such a mammoth and intricate task until the Lord God downloaded the skills to Noah and his artisans. Today when you see modern ocean liners and tankers that carry people and cargoes across the world like the one called Azura, an P & O Ocean Liner in which the manuscript of this book was being revised during its voyage on the Caribbean Sea; you will remember how all this came about – the original knowledge, the skills set and competencies required were provided and supplied by the Almighty God and it was all granted by His free grace.

There is another aspect to grace which transcends all notions of favour and mercy. This is the spiritual grace. Every natural aspect of grace has its equivalent spiritual counterparts and just as in all cases, the spiritual leads the physical, so do the spiritual grace possesses overt superiority over its natural equivalents.

We have seen how the grace that Noah found in God provided him with skills, competencies and all the materials he needed to build the Ark. But the same grace provided Noah with spiritual insight and ability to see and believe what no one else had ever seen or believed.

With spiritual grace, you become susceptible instinctively to the things of God. There were twelve spies sent to spy out the land of Canaan; ten of these saw giants, impenetrable fortification and insurmountable obstacles that would prevent the Israelites from possessing the land. The Bible says the ten brought up an evil report of the land which they had searched saying: the land through which we have gone to search is a land that eats up the inhabitants thereof; and all the people that we saw in it are men of a great stature. And there we saw the giants, the sons of Anak, which come of the giants, and we were in our own sight as grasshoppers and so we were in their sight. (Numbers 13: 32 – 33).

This is what happens when you do not have the grace of spiritual insight given by God. You see problems where blessings abound, you see a magnified and exaggerated but objectively punic power of men instead of the magnificent glory and overwhelming power of the great Jehovah. In the perception of canal mind, your eyesight would only go as far as your unregenerate mind would allow it. You will see only as man sees and no more.

However not so were Caleb and Joshua; (Numbers 13: 30). The grace of God opened their spiritual eyes to see beyond the intimidating and fearsome giants, impregnable fortress, and mountains of impossibilities. They saw the hand of the Almighty for whom nothing; absolutely nothing was impossible. They knew the promises of God regarding the land of Canaan: that God had known in advance the nature of the obstacles and problems the children of Israel would have to surmount and the ferocious battle the sons of Abraham would have to fight with the giants. They knew that the God who had made the promise to give them the land was more, much more able to make good His promises. They recalled in their hearts the unbelievable miracles this wonderful God had performed in the past. How He had delivered the Israelites from the slavery of Pharaoh after having performed differing powerful and unbelievable mighty acts to demonstrate His power. They remembered how Pharaoh had been compelled to voluntarily allow the Israelites to gain their freedom. The God that could do all that and then subsequently destroyed the same Pharaoh and his mighty army in the parted sea, they concluded the same God could very easily defeat the Canaanite giants and they were completely right!

They saw the power of the Almighty God and by grace they knew that nothing, but nothing was impossible for the Almighty to achieve and they said so publicly. The Spirit of grace revealed to them (Caleb & Joshua) the eternal truth that the weapons of our warfare are not carnal, but mighty through God to the pulling down of strong holds; casting down imaginations, and every high thing that exalts itself against the knowledge of God and bringing into captivity every thought to the obedience of Christ (2 Corinthians 10: 4 – 5). "And Joshua the son of Nun and Caleb the son of Jephunneh, which were of them that searched the land rent their clothes and they told the children of Israel saying: the land which we passed through to search it, is an exceeding good land". "If the Lord delight in us, then he will bring us into this land and give it to us; a land which flows with milk and honey. Only do not rebel against the Lord, neither fear ye the people of the land; they are bread for us: their defence is departed from them, and the Lord is with us: fear them not" (Numbers 14: 8 – 10).

The rest of the nation of Israel disagreed and went along with the evil majority report of the ten spies who did not have faith in God due to lack of grace. It is significant to note here that in the eyes of the Lord lack of faith in God is tantamount to rebellion and rebellion and disobedience is regarded by God as idolatry. Idolatry is denying the true and faithful God the honour and adoration due to His wonderful name as God Almighty. This evil behaviour is the same as serving idols. That is why when King Saul was sent to go and destroy the Amalekites (1 Sam 15) and he was specifically instructed not to take any spoil of war but to totally wipe out anything that he saw, or he came into contact with. Saul destroyed only those things that he thought were worthless but kept those things he thought were precious assets to him contrary to the instructions that came directly from God. King Saul was subsequently told in no unmistakable term that his action constituted a rebellion against God – an action similar in nature to idolatry. For this reason, King Saul was rejected by God as king and was replaced by King David. In the same manner, the ten unbelieving spies and the overwhelming majority of the children of Israel who colluded with them in their unbelief; they all subsequently perished in the wilderness according to the word of the Lord. Only

Caleb and Joshua made it to the Promised Land (Number 14: 30).

We see in the story of Noah the work of God's grace. Notice how although it was Noah alone that found grace with God, nevertheless all members of his immediate and extended families were included in the dispensation of mercy. Not only that but even the lives of the animals were spared and preserved for the sake of Noah. This is because the grace of God is flexible, scalable, and inexhaustible and it increases exponentially to cover and deliver the whole of the purposes of God.

Today as it was in the days of Noah, another calamity is about to engulf the world, the current descendants of the Noah humanity are facing extinction because of the same reason that led to the wiping out of the original Adam's evil and recalcitrant humanity - sin. Jesus, God the Son said that as it was in the days of Noah so shall it be also in the days of the Son of man (Luke 17: 26). What were they doing in the time of Noah? They were eating, drinking, and getting married and were giving in marriage until the day that Noah entered into the ark, and the flood came and destroyed them all. (Luke 17:27). Then as now, the word of the Lord was held with levity and contempt, and nobody cared about the need to seek the Lord let alone to serve Him. It was taken for granted that just because no one had ever seen the rain before and there had never been flood, therefore there would never be rain and there would never be flood. Noah must indeed have sounded and looked like a prophet of doom and accordingly held in derision – an amiable fool, a disagreeable fellow, and a figure of fun.

Today we see the similarities with what happened in the days of Noah; because the situation has not changed at all, if anything the situation has enormously got worse; people today are lovers of themselves rather than lovers of God. Even though like in the days of Noah they were severely warned of the impending danger of eternal damnation and destruction, it did not seem to make any difference either to their thinking or their lifestyle choices. It is noticeable that the Ark of Salvation was not put in a hidden place, where no one could see it. The people at the time of Noah witnessed the construction of the boat, indeed some of them were hired to work on constructing the boat of salvation. In so far as we could make out, there were no restrictions preventing anybody from entering the Ark both prior to the beginning of the rain that led to the flood or even whilst it was raining before it became a destructive body of water. Right up to the last minutes, the way of salvation and doors to deliverance, grace and mercy were still left wide open to all until suddenly God Himself at last came to shut the doors and only then was the fate of the recalcitrant and unbelieving sinners finally sealed for all eternity. We are not told how long it took Noah and his Team of engineers to complete the construction of the boat in the boatyard but considering the enormity of the task facing the amateur ship building craftsmen in terms of its size and the intended cargo, it would be reasonable to assume that the task would have taken a good number of years to complete. The fact of the matter is you cannot build a boat without inventing and manufacturing the various pieces of equipment and tools that would be required to build the boat to its original specification. Each of the equipment must have been specially made tools created and needed for skilled craftsmanship work. Our God is the greatest craftsman of precision engineering. Furthermore, it is reasonable to assume that those employed to build the boat must have had to undertake some apprenticeship training to acquire the knowledge and skills required to build the boat. Whilst all these were going on, the warning to repent and the proclamation of mercy of God were being constantly and loudly announced publicly and such announcements were being constantly ignored with equal measure of nonchalance, mockery, and recalcitrance.

Just as the case is today when the word of the Lord the necessity of repentance is received with derision and incredulity and God is mocked and His salvation of free grace and mercy is rejected; so, it was in the days of Noah. It is a matter for regret that those who worked on the boatyard building the boat did not subsequently benefit from the safety and the salvation the boat offered. It is indeed a sad truth that not all who worked for the King in His vineyard would benefit from their labour on the day of the great Harvest.

We do not know the length of time God gave to Noah to warn the people of his days of their impending doom, but we can be sure that knowing our God as a righteous, loving, and holy God, that our God would have given the people of Noah's day more than ample time to repent and a plenty of opportunity to escape the deluge of destruction.

The most holy God has decided to permanently end the sickening, overwhelming wickedness, ingratitude and the brazen arrogance of man. The Almighty God has decided to settle account with humanity and bring its reign to an end permanently. But He has also provided a way out, a cover and protection, an escape route for those desiring salvation from this most certain impending destruction – exactly as He did in the days of Noah when He provided the boat of salvation.

He has provided this time, a greater than the righteous Noah. He has also provided a new expandable boat of deliverance of infinite proportions with inexhaustible capacity to take in those willing to flee from the wrath to come. The Lord Jesus the Saviour and the Redeemer of the mankind has warned that as it was in the days of Noah so would it be when the Son of Man's second coming arrived. The Bible says, where sin abounds, the grace to overcome and neutralize sin and its disastrous consequences abounds greater still (Romans 5:20). This biblical truth is made manifest much more glaringly in the God's new provision for the salvation of humanity. In the first global destruction, Noah was used as a beacon of light of a very narrow restriction and a very limited sanctuary for the perishing humanity. The sanctuary and the protection from destruction provided by Noah was extremely limited – a mere forty-day deliverance from the floods and so was the scope of his ministry.

There was no record to show that Noah ever interceded for the people of his days or any evidence of his pleading for mercy before God for the perishing humanity of his time. The gospel of Noah in so far as one can see was restricted, exclusive and severely limited in scope to within the narrow confines of his immediate family members. The ministry of Noah was a nepotistic dispensation of no value to those outside of his small immediate family circle. It was also a ministry of condemnation, legalism, and judgment without mercy. We were not told what happened after Noah's boat had reached its destination. Although the human cargo had escaped the destruction by the flood, nothing much extraordinary had happened to them during their voyage and probably with the possible exception of Noah himself; the people remained just the same as they were before they boarded the boat. They were ordinary regular people in no way different in character and nature to those who had perished in the flood. They were saved not because of their righteousness or holiness, but only on the basis of their relationship with Noah, the man of grace. Only those who had relationship with grace survived the flood, they were saved only by grace. In other words, even back then in the time of Noah salvation was exclusively secured only on grounds of grace and NOT by work. This is the wisdom of God and here lies another example of the audacity of grace, now as then it was the 'relationship' with the man of grace that provided guarantee for salvation. Here we see some uncanny similarities between the limited and restricted ministry of Noah and the wider much more eternally excellent ministry of the real 'Man of Grace' – God the son, the Lord Jesus Christ.

Today as it was in the days of Noah, salvation is to be procured through the Lord Jesus Christ by grace. However, in God's new plan for human survival and eternal life, a totally wonderful and extremely amazing display of humongous mercy of unimaginable proportions such as the world or even the heaven – indeed the whole realm of creation have never witnessed was unfolded.

In the great plan of God, the very source of all human calamities is to be attacked and destroyed permanently and forever along with his perverse rebellion against God. The new Noah will not be an ordinary man of flesh. He will be mighty God Himself – wow! The new mighty Noah will have both the infinite power and inexhaustible authority over all creation - the heavens and the earth. He will be called: wonderful, Councillor, Prince of peace, the Everlasting Father and God Almighty! (Isaiah 9: 6). The greater Noah will not need anyone to help him build the boat. This is because He Himself will be the boat of salvation as well as the Saviour and the Redeemer. He will have an infinite power and capacity to accommodate all those who desperately and genuinely desire salvation despite the hopelessness of their condition and the filthiness of their unworthy character. He will take their sins upon Himself, cleanse them with His blood and become their righteousness. Because He is God Almighty there will be nothing impossible for Him. Hear what the Holy Spirit says about Him: 'And you shall call His name Jesus, [meaning God the Saviour] because He shall save His people from their sin (Matthew 1: 21). This Saviour and Redeemer God will operate and offer free, comprehensive, and precious grace to all who come to Him, and He will safe them for all eternity regardless of their sins and filthiness.

Noah was only an instrument of salvation but not a Saviour. But Jesus Christ, God the Son is both salvation and the mighty Saviour. Today the whole of humanity are all beneficiaries of grace. What then are the implications of these phenomena? Grace is only available from God the Son and therefore if you are reading this book and you either do not know the Lord Jesus Christ or if you know Him but somehow you have allowed your love for Him to cool down to a freezing point, it is time NOW for you to seek the Lord fervently with fasting, prayer and repentance if necessary.

CHAPTER 3
THE PRACTICAL GRACE

We are returning to look more closely at the issue of grace. We said in the previous chapter how Noah found grace in the eyes of the Lord and that grace which he found led not only to his but to his family survival whilst all others perished in the flood that engulfed the earth and wiped out all living creatures – Genesis 6: 8.

The story of Noah is full of variety of cryptic symbolisms, we see the true roots of the meaning of grace and the unfathomable love and mercy of God as well as the extraordinary length God would go under the covenant of grace. In grace we see the intricacies, complexity as well as the simplicity of the Almighty God at work. Grace uncovers the hidden part, hidden that is to the carnal understanding and the natural knowledge of men; the fundamental and the profound goodness of God – grace exposes the limitless and the unsearchable Father heart of God. In grace, we are beginning to understand with the help of the Holy Spirit the bottomless depth of the loving nature of God.

In the book of Genesis, we see vaguely the divine plan and purposes of God for humanity. We see the love of the Father God in His relationship with Adam before the fall. The Most Mighty and holy God would come down to visit Adam and would walk around with him in the Garden of Eden like a loving father would walk with his precious child. They would exchange greetings and pleasantries and God would give a new present on each visit He made to Adam – some new breed of animals or birds or fishes that God has made in His latest creation; He would ask Adam to name these creatures and whatever names Adam gave the creatures became their names for ever.

It is like a father going to Wal-Mart Supermarket in America or Tesco Supermarket in England or a Shoprite Supermarket in Nigeria on their way home from work to buy present to give to their child at home and when they have done so to experience the joy that the child would feel when her father gives the gift to his daughter and then watches with utter joy the daughter experiences the delight of her father's affection and love.

The picture that emerges from this scenario is that of a loving father seeking relationship with his child, having a deep, personal one to one relationship of an intimate nature with his beloved child. This is exactly the kind of relationship God the Father had with Adam and it is exactly the same kind of relationship He craves with you.

The love and care of God for His children is so extraordinary. You can just imagine the Father God leaving His resplendent glory and palatial throne with the company of billions of mighty Angels worshipping and honouring Him with most exquisite music of heaven and abandoning all the splendour and glory of all the heavens have to offer just for the sake of having a one to one rendezvous with Adam in a lonely Garden. It is a loud statement and a wonderful majestic proclamation of God's order of priorities. Apparently all the glory of the universes, the beauty of heavens, the wonders of all creation, the milky ways and the billions and billions of myriad bodies, the Sun, the stars, the moons and countless wonders of God's beautiful and amazing creation; the most important to God was Adam! The heart of God and the centre of His affection and love was Adam. The intensity of God's lavish affection for Adam is revealed for all to see here; all God's visit to Adam was conducted solo and unaccompanied by the Arch Angels – not a single Angel was allowed to intrude. The Garden itself became an hallowed and holy ground because of the presence of the Almighty God and His love child, Adam. Child of God, the Father God has not changed, His nature and character never changes. Your Father God lives and occupies the position of everlasting and perpetual perfection: He cannot increase in any shape or form and neither can He ever decrease either in wisdom, power, authority or majesty in perpetuity. He is God Almighty, omniscient, omnipresent and omnipotent. What He did to Adam is exactly what He wants to do with you. And just as He loved Adam that much, the same way He loves you and just as much as He tried to have a close and intimate relationship with Adam, the same He wants to have a close, productive and intimate loving relationship with you. The point I am trying to make is that in exactly the same way Adam was loved unconditionally and was very highly regarded by God before the fall of Adam, so does the Lord God the Father loves you and have a very high regard for you as an apple of His eyes.

Let no one deceive you into believing that you are nothing to God and that He does not care for you or about what happens to you. Hear what He says: "Can a mother forget her nursing baby that she would not show love to it?" yet the mother would forget when she is asleep. But your Father God never sleeps or slumbers! (Isaiah 49:15). The child of God, the Lord has not forsaken you and He will never do. Why then you may ask are things are like what they are for me? The answer is you may not have been listening to the Lord's instructions or keeping His words in your life. Listen to what the Almighty says: "Take hold of my words which all your heart, keep my commands and you will live" (Proverbs 4: 4-5). Our God is non-partial God who steadfastly keeps to His words and His promises with meticulous and unflinching integrity.

We do not know how long this blessed and intimate relationship between God and Adam went on for, because the Bible did not indicate the length of time before the fall. However, there is no doubt that the experience for both parties was mutually beneficial. The grace of God created a friendship and relationship between the great and

Almighty God and an ordinary mortal in the form of an insignificant Adam. This is an approximation of the intense intimacy between God and Adam. Here is an amazing fact of the story; the Almighty God of all creation would walk side by side with Adam as they tour the beautiful Garden together. I am inclined to believe that this walk-about was the real manifestation of the intense love God had for Adam. Because although the Bible does not say that Adam saw God face to face nevertheless, it is very clear this regular get together was the biggest highlight of the day for both God and Adam before Eve was created. You could imagine this, and you could picture yourself walking in a sublimely beautiful Garden hand in hand with the Almighty God the Creator of the whole universe? Yet this was exactly what happened in the Garden of Eden between God and His Adam.

This is a demonstration and a confirmation of the kind of relationship the Almighty had in mind for His children before the Fall and before the calamity of disobedience destroyed the wonderful and the harmoniously beautiful relationship between God and Adam.

This close and intense intimacy the Father God had with Adam was unique in creation. We know this because God never replicated such relationship with anyone else outside the Trinity. The Bible makes it very clear that the Angels regardless of rank were not allowed to participate in this kind of one-to-one relationship with God – such was the exclusivity and love in this divine intense intimacy. Furthermore, we know that even in God's heavenly throne room Angels regardless of their ranks are not allowed to behold the face of the Almighty; they have to cover their faces when they are in the presence of God otherwise, they would be consumed by the resplendent power of the glory of God. By this we can see how very privileged and highly regarded Adam was in the eyes of the living and the Most High God.

Here again we see the practical evidence of the audacity of grace which enabled Adam, a mere mortal to enjoy such a close and exclusive affinity with the Almighty God.

Now the Paradise which was lost to Adam because of the treachery, disobedience and betrayal has been regained for us by the Lord Jesus Christ the Saviour and the Redeemer of the mankind, this grace concession denied to Adam because of sin has now been fully restored to us through Christ. This wonderful and excellent news means we are now able to reconnect with God our Father and resume the same intense intimate relationship which our Father had enjoyed with Adam in the Garden of Eden before the fall. The former partition and the dividing walls separating us from God has now been bridged by the deeds of mercy of Jesus Christ and the grand and everlasting sacrifice that He made of himself as God the Son; the highly exalted and divine High Priest to satisfy the righteousness of the Living God.

We can now boldly come before the Throne of God expectantly to claim and receive the promises and the blessings of God in good and satisfying measure. The grace procured by Jesus Christ the Son of God, the

Redeemer and Saviour of the mankind is so full, so all encompassing and so comprehensive that it covers all aspects of our lives from the cradle to the grave and even beyond. The Bible says all God's promises are yes and amen in the Lord Jesus Christ (2 Corinthians 1:20); and nothing but nothing would the Father now withhold from us His children who had been bought and cleansed by the precious blood of the Lord and Saviour Jesus Christ. The Apostle Paul puts it very succinctly and beyond any reasonable doubt when he declared that if the Almighty God did not shrink back from giving us His only begotten Son, then there is nothing else, He would not freely give to us (John 3:16). Why is this very significant? It is very significant because of all that the Almighty God possesses in heaven, on the earth and in myriad of universes and galaxies and dominions, none is more important or more precious to Him than His very own precious Son. We know this because time and again in the New Testament, we see the personal affirming witness statements from God the Father Himself: This is my beloved Son in whom I am well pleased (Mathew 3:17); this is my beloved Son, hear Him (Matthew 17: 5). The greatness of and the importance of the Lord Jesus Christ to God cannot be overemphasized. Moses the Great, told the Jews of his days that God was going to raise up in Israel a prophet who would have the word of God and everyone must listen to this great Prophet; otherwise they would be held to account for disobedience to his words. (Deuteronomy 18:18 – 19) Furthermore, the importance of Jesus is that He is referred to as God the Son whilst God is called God the Father. The essence of this reference is to draws attention to the incontrovertible fact that both God the Father and God Son are essentially ONE and indivisible both in nature, in essence and in characteristics.

Listen to the description given by the Bible to the nature of Christ: for unto us a child (of God) is born, unto us a Son (of God) is given; and the government shall be upon His shoulder; and His name shall be called Wonderful, Counsellor, The mighty God, The everlasting Father, The Prince of Peace. (Isaiah 9:6). Please note the reference to the title 'Mighty God' given in relation to the Lord Jesus Christ. Later, more emphatically God the Son Himself declared: My Father and I are One (John 10:30). Later at the direction of the Holy Spirit, Saint Paul talking about the same subject of oneness and indivisibility of God the Son and God the Father said this: who is the image of the invisible God, the first born of every creature: For by him were all things created that are in heaven, and that are in earth, visible and invisible, whether they be thrones, or dominions, or principalities, or dominions, or principalities, or powers, all things were created by Him and for Him (Colossians 1:15 – 16).

Saint Paul further elaborated this in his epistle to the Philippians in chapter 2. "Let this mind be in you which was also in Christ Jesus: who being in the form of God, thought it not robbery to be equal with God. But made Himself of no reputation and took upon Himself the form of a servant and was made in the likeness of men: And being found in fashion as a man, he humbled Himself and became obedient unto death, even the death on the cross" (Philippians 2: 5 – 8).

In a straightforward language, what this means is that Jesus Christ, God the Son is of the same substance with God the Father in a relationship where God the Son though of equal status with the Father nevertheless voluntarily conceded supremacy and precedence to God the Father. Furthermore, God the Son deliberately chose to take upon Himself the role of a servant with willingness to observe a full, active and total obedience to His Father's will including obedience unto death on the cross (Philippians 2: 8).

What this implies is very staggering, indeed too implausible to contemplate. If God the Son is of the same substance as God the Father, it means God the Father was not an innocent bystander in the business of salvation, reconciliation, and redemption of humanity; put simply, God the Father and God the Son and God the Holy Spirit had in eternity past decided and concluded the 'Redemption Plan' for humanity – even well before the humanity was ever created!

So, throughout the earthly ministry of Christ, the Trinity was actively and consistently present as one indivisible force. When God the Son suffered, God the Father suffered and when God the Son was dying on the cross, God the Father was there with Him and the only time God the Son was ever alone was at the point when all the sins of the world were heaped upon Him and God the Father had to forsake His Son because it was impossible for the holiness and purity of God the Father to tolerate sin. It was the unbearable pain of this separation between God the Father and God the Son even though it was of temporary duration, that led to the broken heart on the part of the God the Son, and it was this broken heart caused by separation that ultimately led to the death of the Lord Jesus Christ, the Saviour and Redeemer of the mankind.

You can see now how important the Lord Jesus Christ was before He decided to take on the task of becoming the Saviour and Redeemer of the mankind. And through this, you can also see how solid and sure your salvation is because of the integrity and the utter righteousness of the active Trinity who played varying role in bringing about this precious and wonderful salvation. But that is not all: the salvation purchased by the precious blood of God the Son is to be given out free of charge to all sinful and unworthy men without merit through grace induced faith. What a God and how great indeed the love the Father has for us that led Him to give us His Only Son who by all account is the most precious of all to Him.

CHAPTER 4
RESTARTING AFRESH WITH GRACE

We are continuing with the subject of grace and in this Chapter we want to explore restarting afresh with grace in our daily lives. Many people are very realistic about the moral failings and character deficiencies in their daily lives. A lot of people have had their lives destroyed and their either to glistering careers ruined because of their character frailties and habits that have become so deeply ingrained in their psyche that has permanently and negatively altered their personality to the detriment of their long term interest. This is a fundamental matter of life and death.

There is a popular proverb that says that "manners maketh man". The kind of manners that you exhibit in your relationship with others is an objective indication of the kind of man or woman you are. Very rarely is a man or woman entirely and irredeemably bad in all their manifestations – except of course by comparison to the standards of holiness and righteousness of God.

Nevertheless the best of us have their 'bad turns' blind spots of moral inadequacies. Some wise ones among us would try to change by attempting to adopt a compensatory lifestyle that mar or veil our character weaknesses. This fig leaf very rarely works! This is because no man can truly change himself. A leopard cannot change his spots.

Moral failings are natural attributes of unregenerate mind and the heart that has not been submitted to God. The Bible is full of the account of human moral failings and weaknesses of many famous characters. Notable examples of these are Samson and King David. The strongest man that has ever lived, Samson went too far in his reckless addiction to inordinate sexual practices and ended up being put under the judgement of God. In his unguarded hours of moral weakness, he revealed and betrayed the secret of his God-given supernatural strength to his ardent and blood thirsty enemies through a forbidden sexual desire and illicit love of a strange woman called Delilah (Judges 16:16-19).

Samson was consequently stripped of his supernatural power and strength; he was subsequently captured by his sworn enemies; had his eyes gouged out, turned into a slave, mocked by his captors, and thrown into a Philistine dungeon. Later Samson perished with his captors in a terrible and deliberate disaster under the debris of falling heavy masonry whilst being paraded as object of mockery, ridicule, and fun. All these calamities fell on Samson because of the unguarded areas of his addiction to illegitimate sex and pride! (Judges 16: 18; 20 – 30).

The Bible indicates that King David also struggled with sexual temptation and sin. In a moment of moral weakness David fell prey to the spirit of lust which led him to commit adultery, misuse of power and later an odious state sponsored murder – a set of terrible and inexcusable sins before the Lord (2 Samuel 11: 2 – 17)

But here is a crucial and most surprising difference, David did not die in prison or held in public derision and shame like Samson. David instead died a national hero of the heaven and the earth; he died according to the heaven's account of his life: 'a man after God's own heart' Wow! What made the difference? David repented of his terrible sins and made a fresh start with God. In brokenness and full humility David called on the Lord and his genuine repentance and fulsome confession of his sin before God. This display of genuine penitence led to total forgiveness from God and David's restoration to favour. In addition to this, God extended His grace to David to carry on as if nothing had happened at all. What a God of mercy and grace is our Father God (2 Samuel 12: 13).

Here we clearly see the attitude of our loving, caring, merciful and generous God. The sins of these two Bible characters were committed in secret – but as we all know there is nothing secret with God, whatever a man sows, so shall he reap and what is more all unforgiven sins shall be accounted for because your sins shall find you out (Numbers 32: 23) no ifs, no buts. The Bible is very clear about this: your Father who sees you in secret shall reward you openly.

So, what are the implications of these facts: I have been sent to warn you that your sins shall find you out and there is no hiding place for sinners in the presence of God. I must therefore ask you to please stop and ask yourself a pertinent question: 'Am I living a secret double life that only God and I know about? Have you allowed yourself like Samson to become so addicted to your secret sin that you have convinced yourself to believe there is no possibility of turning back? I have been sent to tell you that this is not the case and to offer you a rethink in the name of God of Jacob. It is never too late to start doing what is right; it is never too late to stop serving Satan. You cannot sink so deep that Christ is unable to lift you out of your dungeon of sins and depravity. Repentance is the key here. Repentance is the place to start as David did. This entails you having to confess your sins, turning away from your sins and failure, and acknowledging your inability to change on your own. But you must certainly stop finding excuses for your sins, and stop, full stop rationalising what you are doing – otherwise you are just fooling and deceiving yourself. You may have kept your sins secret so far, but ultimately as I said earlier you will invariably be found out (2 Samuel 12: 12).

I am pleading with you to do exactly what David did. He cried out to God with an utter sincerity; listen to what he said 'Cleanse me from my sin, create in me a pure heart Oh God: (Psalm 51: 2;10). First David recognised the need to admit his sins before God. Furthermore, he recognised that his heart was impure and more importantly, he also recognised that he could under no circumstances help to erase the filthiness of his immoral heart and Godless lifestyle. The recognition of these truths led him to humbly seek the mercy of God with a broken heart and sincerity. Note that David did not seek to justify himself or resorted to some extenuating circumstances or lame excuses to explain away his wicked deeds. He did not minimise the enormity of his wickedness neither did he seek refuge under the divine rights and the absolutism of his Kingship. David was brutally honest with himself by submitting himself to God in true penitence and unrestricted repentance. The God of mercy and grace looked down from His throne and saw David's penitent heart and He forgave him his sins and delivered him from his utter wretchedness.

Again here we see the God of grace in action. Grace does not treat sin with levity, God is an utterly holy God who cannot abide sin in whatever form and treats sins as egregious infractions against His holy law. Grace looks to and facilitates reconciliation and redemption through Jesus Christ the great Redeemer of the Mankind. Grace acknowledges the sinful and the falling nature of man; it accepts God's justification in judging the sinners because the law of God is perfect and our God is utterly just and wholly righteous in all His ways. However grace sees beyond the guilt; sees beyond sin and beyond the condemnation that accompanies sin and the terrible damage it does to God/man relationship. Grace transcends judgment and its ministry of condemnation that Satan has brought to humanity. In Adam as well as in Moses, we are all guilty under the law, because the law was given through Moses and therefore the judgment that results for breaking the law; but grace and truth came through Jesus Christ, the Saviour of mankind (John 1:17).

The supreme sacrifice made by the Lord Jesus Christ has ushered in God's unmerited mercy which paved the way for us all to be justified through the redemption that came through Jesus Christ alone (Romans 3:24).

The importance of grace is graphically illustrated by the lives of these two men: David and Samson. Both were fallible men, both were anointed by God and both were God appointed leaders of Israel. The two men were guilty of the same sin of adultery but whilst one – Samson paid dearly for his indiscretion with disastrous consequences which led to his death of shame and dishonour; the other man, David who actually committed a more grievous and abominable sin against the Lord escaped punishment unscathed. Why was this seemingly double standard allowed by God? The intervention of grace made the difference! Similarly both Judas Iscariot and Simon Peter committed the same terrible sin of denying their Lord; whilst Judas Iscariot condemned himself to death through suicide; Peter was pardoned and subsequently made one of the principal leaders of the first Century Church of God – a great honour indeed!

Again we ask why was it possible for one to receive the mercy of God and unmerited pardon whilst the other was made to face the full rigour of the consequences of sin and judgment. Grace intervened! Grace provided the circumstances by providing an opportunity which invokes the righteousness and the justice of God and made compelling case leading to the cancellation of judgment and its consequences against both David and Simon Peter – grace induced repentance!

Repentance is an attitude of the heart that is pleasing to the Almighty God. The Holy Spirit makes this very clear, "repent ye therefore and be converted that your sin may be blotted out and the time of refreshing may come from the Lord" (Acts 3:19)

After Job had come to himself, he repented of his self-righteousness "therefore I despise myself and repent in dust and ashes" (Job 42:6).

The central point of Jesus Ministry was the proclamation of His Kingdom and the necessity for repentance as an absolute prerequisite "they went out and preached that people should repent" (Mark 6:12). To be absolutely clear it is only in the finished work of Christ alone that salvation is found for humanity. However this work of Christ which includes His words, His totally sinless sacrificial life and the shedding of His most precious blood as atonement for sin is predicated on accepting Jesus Christ first and foremost as Lord and Saviour.

Salvation is by grace alone, the grace of the Lord Jesus Christ. It is by grace that a sinner is convicted of the need for salvation and compelled by the Holy Spirit to come to faith in the Lord Jesus Christ. However the grace that brings you to the Lord Jesus Christ is the same grace that will sustain you throughout your journey here on earth. If you are experiencing the problems of moral failings and character deficiencies, take the problem by faith to the Lord Jesus Christ in an earnest and sustained prayer and ask for His grace to overcome. Jesus Christ is not only the salvation provider but He is also the great Deliverer. The Angel told Mary that "You shall call His name Jesus, (God the Saviour) because He shall save His people from their sin" (Matthew 1: 21). This means the sovereign Lord Jesus will not only save His people from the consequences of sin, but more significantly, He will deliver them from the curse of sinning. The Lord Jesus fulfilled His deliverer's role in Mark 5, when He set free a man from the tyranny of demon possession – (Mark 5:8 – 19). All bad behaviour and character deficiencies have satanic underpinnings which are the instigating factors that cause the captive people to sin and behave in manners that are manifestly detrimental to their own interest just like the man who was delivered by the Lord.

Many Christians are not aware of this truth: Jesus Christ is a total Saviour and the absolute Deliverer from the powers and principalities of the Satanic dominion. He does not only have the power to give you eternal life, He also has the power and the authority to sustain, protect and deliver you from all evils here on earth. Jesus is an all-round Saviour, Defender, Protector, Deliverer and Provider. He has the power through grace to order an end to your sinful nature and transform your life and your nature to that resembling the nature of God. The Bible says that sin shall no longer be your master; because you are not under the law anymore but now under grace (Romans 6:14).

When you have faithfully given all your heart to Jesus Christ; you must take another crucial step – you need to ask the Lord Jesus to come into your life and ask Him to wash you with His precious blood. Then you need to look for a Church where the true word of God is preached, and Jesus Christ is honoured and become part of the fellowship there. Do not try to battle alone to defeat sin in your life, make a fresh start with God by making new friends and acquaintances with the local Christian Church. You will find that a fresh start with God in the company of other genuine Christians will yield great dividends in terms of rapid change for the betterment of your life.

CHAPTER 5
GOD HAS PLAN FOR YOUR LIFE

> "I know the thoughts that I think of you."
>
> — *JEREMIAH 29: 11*

We human beings always want to know what the future holds for us and although we do not have the ability to accurately foretell the future with precise details this has not stopped us from wanting to try. This instinct for curiosity is totally understandable - if we can be sure of the future; then we can plan our lives in such a way that will enable us to avoid the pitfalls and vicissitudes of life. This explains why fortunes are spent annually on fortune telling and soothsayers. However, as Christians our lives are hidden in Christ who not only knows the future but controls it meticulously.

The other thing people do at the beginning of the year is take stock of their achievements in the previous year and then make a dramatic gesture of drawing up a list of behaviour patterns that have not served them well in the preceding years; they then resolve to make changes that will lead them to do better in the coming months of the New Year. This is called the New Year Resolution. Unfortunately, this strong resolve to turn a new leaf and change for the better is normally very short lived because it does not work. No sooner are the so-called New Resolutions made than they are broken and the people are forced to resort back to their status quo a few weeks after the Resolutions have been made with fanfare.

The fact of the matter is that men and women do not possess the ability to change themselves for the better without the help of God. The Bible specifically asks the salient question: Can the leopard change his spots? (Jeremiah 13: 23) The Bible is categorical that those who are accustomed to doing evil cannot unilaterally by their own effort of self will and strong determination change for the better. You need far more than inner strength and self determination to change yourself.

The only New Year Resolution that is worth having is the one where a clear decision has been taken to seek God through Jesus Christ in spirit and in truth. It is only then the power of God through the work of the Holy Spirit comes into your life and genuinely changes you fundamentally from within by washing you in the precious blood of the Lord Jesus Christ, washing your sins away and transferring you from the kingdom of darkness into the Kingdom of Light by the grace of the Lord Jesus Christ the Saviour and the Redeemer of Mankind. The Bible says only this can make you a new person with God given ability through the power of the Holy Spirit to be transformed into a much better person. The Bible says therefore if any man be in Christ, he is a new creature: old things are passed away; behold all things are become new (2 Corinthians 5:17).

Indeed, we are further told that a man is not justified by the works of the law– i.e., by being good according to the human definition of what constitutes goodness. We are only justified by faith in the Lord Jesus Christ alone and that only by grace. (Galatians 2:16).

When you truly know and properly understand the true God, the Father of our Lord Jesus Christ it is not the future that you need to worry about but the present. Why? Because it is the present that matters; it is the present that determines what the future holds in store. Amazingly, God has been very candid with us His creation on what we can expect the future to look like. Indeed, we are given the ability to influence directly what our future looks like to a very considerable degree. The Bible says whatever a man sows in the present is exactly what he will in future reap (Galatian 6:7). This means if we want a better future for ourselves, we must today sow the seeds that are capable of producing the kind of future we envisage for ourselves and our children tomorrow. But there are areas of our lives where there are factors and circumstances that are invariably outside of our control. So, when we are faced with situations like these, it is then that our relationship with God kicks in.

Our faith in God and our unflinching believe in His utter goodness will reassure our hearts and minds that our God is for us and not against us. Indeed, the Bible says 'in all your ways acknowledge Him and He shall direct your paths (Proverbs 3: 6).

So, the question is - are you ready to safeguard your future with absolute certainty? I have been sent to tell you that you can today secure a better future for yourself – a future filled with an absolute certainty of God's blessings, joy, and happiness and be guaranteed of God's protection, care, and support. Hear what God says in the scripture: I know the thought that I think of you, it is the thought of good and not of evil, to give you a future and a hope (Jeremiah 29: 11).

As somebody who has had the privilege of knowing God, I can tell you most assuredly that our God is a promise keeping God with unflinching integrity and righteousness. I can assure you that based on what He has done in my life; He is a God that will do exactly as He said He would. When you genuinely give your life to God you will discover that He will take over the running of your life going forward. The Bible tells us that the steps of a good man or woman are ordered by the Lord, and He is delighted in their way (Psalms 37: 23). If in the New Year you were to give your life to Christ, you will discover a fundamental change within yourself and your circumstances.

You will watch in awe as defeats in your life give way to victory and you will see how impossibilities become possible as you go forward in the Lord and in His power of resurrection. You will come to realise that those who wait upon the Lord shall renew their strength; they shall run and not be weary and they shall mount up with wings as eagles and they shall walk and not faint (Isaiah 40:31). You will see the qualitative difference between the previous aimless self-centred life you have lived before, and the exciting new life based on the love of God. You will be able to testify with your own life experiences that those who know their God shall be strong and do great exploits (Daniel 11: 32).

CHAPTER 6
PRACTICAL CHRISTIANITY
PART 1

In this chapter, we are going to explore Christianity and what it takes to be a Christian. But before we do that, we must first explain what Christianity is and how it came about. We are of course going to depend on the only legitimate source of historical truth. The Bible is the inerrant word of God and the final authority on how humanity should live [John 10:35, John 17:17]

The roots of Christianity sprang from God Himself. Every nation on the earth was an idol worshipper and God decided to reveal Himself by establishing personal relationship with humanity. He chose Abraham an Iraqi Arab Idol worshipper from the Ur of the Chaldees [Genesis 12:1–3] with whom to establish a personal relationship that will eventually impact the whole of humanity. Abraham became the father of faith and patriarch for those who believe in one true God. Later God extended the relationship to include the descendants of Abraham, the Jewish people now called Israel who He chose for Himself.

God gave Moses the premier Jewish Prophet and leader the Ten Commandments to regulate and govern human relations. The law of Moses paved the way to the increased awareness of sin and the penalties for breaking the law of God [Exodus 20:1-17]. The human inability to keep the law of God leads to man being alienated and estranged from God. The relationship with man broke down because sin increased, and man had no answer to the problem of sin. And yet God had declared that every soul that sins shall die and be separated for ever from God.

But God is merciful. Although God is holy and the human's inability to keep the law means that judgement must follow nevertheless God found a way to safe man from the consequences of his action. He sent Jesus Christ to die on the cross to pay for our sin. In return for this substitutionary death on the Cross by the Lord Jesus, anyone who comes to God through Him shall be saved for ever. Furthermore, there is no other way to God, no not one except through Jesus Christ. This is the reason why the Bible says in John 3:16. 'For God so loved the world that He sent His only begotten Son that whosoever believes in Him should not perish but have eternal life. It was further clearly stated that anyone who does not believe in the Son of God is condemned already [John 3:18]. So those who accept the Lord Jesus as Son of God and believe that His blood shed on the Cross washes their sins away and are prepared to follow and keep the law of

God through the grace given by Jesus Christ are called Christians.

Please notice the definition used here. Christians are not necessarily those who have Christian names or those who are born into a Christian home. Christianity is not something you inherit; Yes for sure you can inherit Christian culture and customs if your born or brought up in a Christian home and in a nominal Christian country. However, none of this makes you a Christian, this is because Christianity is NOT a religion it is a relationship and a covenant between God and you; it is something you go into as a deliberate choice without compulsion and with full unflinching commitment. Christianity is unique; it is not like any of the religions that you see every day. All religions are no more than rituals and sets of rules set up as systems of social control created by humans and for humans. Christianity is different: it is NOT a religion, but a relationship between God and those who love and serve Him through faith in the Lord Jesus Christ the Saviour and Redeemer of mankind.

Christianity was originated and validated by God through sending His Son to reveal Himself to humanity. Christianity is the only organized system of worship which calls God the Father; it is the only religion in so far as you can call it a religion that boasts of personal relationship with God. It is the only religion that makes a bold claim of certainty of the history of creation, the purpose of life and the only religion that offers a solid certainty of life after death for those who follow and practise its teaching. It is the only religion whose Head is in heaven and who alone controls the destinies of all creations in heaven and on the earth.

Christianity is unique because it is the only revealed religion that guarantees you peace, success and happiness in life and a total victory in death and after death. Christianity is the only religion that promises and delivers total transformation of your life and turns you into a new creation through the power of the Holy Spirit of God. Indeed, Christianity is the only exclusive and guaranteed way of receiving the Holy Spirit who will guide, strengthen, teach and lead you all the days of your life right through the vicissitudes and manifold dangers of this complex world. It is only in Christianity that a solid promise of protection, power and victory over Satan and his dark forces from the evil realms are offered and guaranteed. In Christianity, you are never alone or abandoned to your own devices, you are given the strength through the Holy Spirit to maintain close and intimate relationship with the Almighty God throughout your days on earth and in all things that you do.

Furthermore, Christianity is not a do it yourself religion, you will be guided to know instinctively what is right and wrong and provided with strength to choose the right course in life by the power of the Holy Spirit. And if you choose to obey the word of God and the leading of the Holy Spirit, when you make mistakes as you are bound to, you will receive help to start up again because your life is no longer about you; it is now offered to God and you have become His child.

All other religions offer work orientation and moral uprightness that their adherents and followers are not able to fulfil or attain, a code of moral excellence that is practically impossible to achieve. In other words they are given a world of perpetual struggle between good and evil; a war that they know they can never win because of the inherent human weaknesses. The Bible is clear about all human righteousness; the best of human righteousness is described as filthy rags before God – a totally useless and wholly unacceptable exercise ( ). God is only interested in the standard of His own holiness and righteousness and this can only be achieved through grace by the power of the Holy Spirit of Jesus Christ the Son of the Most High God.

As said earlier Christians are those who follow Christ and serve Him in truth and in Spirit [John 4:24]; they are called Christians meaning 'little Christs' because like their Master they are beacons of light to the world wherever they live. Their lifestyle reflected the glory of God. Their life is dedicated to serving the true God with reverential fear and genuine love of God. They honour Him not with leap service but with actual living the life of obedience to the law and statutes of God.

Maybe you who are reading this book you are a Christian then you can determine what kind of Christian you are in the light of the word of God. Jesus Christ our Lord and Saviour has categorically stated that He had not come to abolish the law of God but to fulfil it all. He further explains very clearly that without holiness, no one shall see God. This means exactly that unless we who call ourselves Christians abide in our Lord by keeping His law then we are not His followers – it is as simple as that, no ifs and no buts!. There is no middle or independent ground in biblical Christianity; you are either for God totally and unreservedly or you are against Him. Christianity is not a religion for those with a liberal mind-set or those who think man is an end unto himself. Christianity is a religion of total obedience to and reliance on God and His word unquestionably.

If your lifestyle is no different from those who do not know God then, you quite clearly are not Christian. If you are still living in sin without the fear of God, regardless of who you think you are, you are deceiving yourself and you are not a Christian. Maybe you are a Pastor, or an Evangelist, and you are dabbling in sin in a secret lifestyle, and you think you are covered because you are called 'the man of God' and nobody sees you. You are in a position of authority which you abuse persistently to further your selfish sinful desire and exploitative interest. Maybe you sing in a Choir with a voice like that of Canary, but you are living an adulterous lifestyle and holiness is a foreign language to you. You call yourself a Christian but also see yourself as one of the lads with laddish behaviour pattern and foul language that profanes the good name of God. Maybe you are married, a father and head of household, you are a good friendly guy to all in the Church and in the street, but you are a terror at home to your wife and kids.

You are Mr Nice Guy, a heart and soul of the party. People speaking glowingly of your reputation in a fake outward show of pretend godliness – but only you know the life of obscene perversion you live in secret. I am sent to tell you all that you are not a Christian at all and if Christ were to return today you will go to hell along with your belief system.

You see the faith that does not stop you from sinning; that faith is NOT of Christ and it will take you straight to hell. Jesus Christ the only Saviour and Redeemer of mankind says categorically: "I tell you no! But unless you repent, you will all perish! (Luke 13:5). I hear you say but we are saved by grace and not by our work of righteousness, yes you are absolutely right; however the grace that saves us the same grace also that demands that we flee from sin. The same grace provides us with the strength and ability to overcome sin and to serve the Lord by living the life of holiness through the power of the Holy Spirit.

If your Christian life has not yet led you to the transformation of your inner being and you have not yet experienced the great joy of living for God by grace; it is not too late for you to seek the Lord earnestly through repentance. Hear what the Almighty God says "You will seek me and you will find me when you seek me with all your heart (Jeremiah 29:13) So if you now decide to seek the Lord more intimately and genuinely and come back to your first love in genuine repentance, you will find the Lord (Deuteronomy 4:29). The Bible says let not sin therefore reign in your mortal body, that you should obey its lusts thereof [Romans 6:12] but yield yourself to God as instruments of righteousness [Romans 6:13]

It is entirely possible that you who are reading this book, you are not a Christian, and if that is so then today is the happiest day of your life. Everything you have read so far is totally true. Christianity is NOT a religion but a relationship with the One and only true God. Jesus Christ His only begotten Son was sent to die for you. Jesus Christ the Saviour lived a totally sinless and righteous life but was nevertheless crucified like a common criminal for your sin and my sin. There is no salvation anywhere else except through the Lord Jesus Christ the Son of the most high God. All the man-made religions are a waste of time, they are all without exceptions including Islam, the work of the Devil, they are all to differing degrees mimicry and deception: it will not take you anywhere with God because all human righteousness is nothing but filthy rags before God. You can come to God right now and be sure of your eternal salvation through the Lord Jesus Christ with humility and ask Him for forgiveness. Please see the Sinner's prayer on the last chapter of this book.

CHAPTER 7
WHO ARE THE CHRISTIANS?
PART 1

In the last chapter we discussed what practical Christianity entails; this makes clear and answers the question who is a Christian. We explained that Christianity was not man made but it is a religion that sprang up directly from God. Moreover, we reiterated the more important truth that Christianity was not a religion at all but a way of life and a relationship between God and those who love our God and have come to know God through Jesus Christ. We explained at length that salvation and mercy of God came through Jesus Christ the Son of the Most High God alone and that there is no other way acceptable to God for securing God's favour and salvation.

We went on to explain what constitutes true biblical Christianity. We made it clear that whilst faith in Jesus Christ, the Saviour though important and absolutely indispensable, it only forms a part of the essential two steps process required by the Saviour Himself before a person can be truly called a Christian. Jesus said 'if you are my friends, then keep my commandments' [John 15:14]. [Matthew 7:21] Consequently the biblical definition of the true Christian is one who loves The Lord Jesus Christ and keeps His law. As pointed out in previous chapters that anyone who says they are Christian and are engaging in sin are sadly and dangerously misled as Jesus has categorically stated that without righteousness, no one shall see God [Matthew 5:20]

We are going to look at what promises God has made to those who have become reconciled with Him by coming through the Lord Jesus Christ and are cleansed by His precious blood. Firstly, the Bible says there is a joy in heaven when a repentant sinner comes to faith in Jesus Christ [Luke 15:7]. Secondly, the sinner is transformed miraculously by the power of the Holy Spirit, and he/she instantaneously becomes the child of God. His sin however many and regardless of their enormity is washed away by the precious blood of Christ and completely erased and the person then stands in the full righteousness of God as a holy person before the Throne of Grace and God will remember his sin no more because our Lord Jesus Christ has already paid the penalty with His precious life and His most holy blood. God in His grace is fully satisfied.

Furthermore, the person is given the sanctification of God which confirms him as saint (Hebrew 8:10). Because of his new faith in God through Christ's redeeming love, he is instantly adopted into the family of God by God's justification through faith (Romans 3:24) and he can now address God as his Father.

The implications of this stupendous transformation are enormous and are frankly beyond human imagination or description. It means a man has switched sides permanently: from the kingdom of darkness into the kingdom of God. A man previously marked down by sin for certain destruction is now suddenly transformed and has all his sins and doubts wiped away. A man who was previously a slave to sin and horrible perversions, a bond slave of Satan has suddenly been completely redeemed. A new life now begins, the cares of the past, and all the anxieties, worries, guilt, hopelessness all gone: our new man is freed for ever!

The Bible says those who are in Christ are a new creation – all things in the past with their terrible histories of defeats, failures, disappointments; psychological and physical abuses, terrifying injustices, hatred and wickedness of varying descriptions, oppressions, depressions, flagrant disloyalties, and every kind of man's inhumanity against man – are all gone and forgotten and forgiven! A new life of joy unspeakable and full of glory now begins (II Corinthians 5:17).

May be as you read this book, you would like a life like this. Maybe you have never really had any joy in your life, however much you tried. May be what you had thought would bring happiness to your life has turned out to be a shadow. You have worked hard all your life and played hard too in the hope of securing happiness and of course you have tried everything money can buy, beautiful women galore, fine wine, fancy cars, exclusive expensive holidays and palatial mansions in beautiful locations and private jets to match. The more you have, the more you want to possess, and the vicious cycle goes on leaving you without any real joy or meaningful happiness. You see the more you try, the less the satisfaction you derive from all these toys and sinful lifestyles.

I have been sent to tell you that what you need to know that the peace of your soul cannot be bought with money. The joy of life is not to be found in the acquisition of money, more money and materialism. Your soul: that part of your body which is the real you is far more precious than what money or an affluent lifestyle can satisfy. In the same way, your peace of mind and happiness here on earth can only be achieved when you are perfectly aligned with the will and purposes of your maker – the Almighty God. The true peace and joy can only be found in Jesus Christ. Only Jesus Christ can heal the broken hearted. Hear what the Bible says 'come and buy from me without money and without price. Why do you spend your money on that which cannot satisfy?' [Isaiah 55:1-3] [Revelation 21:6] I have been sent to tell you that only Jesus the Saviour can satisfy the yearnings of your heart and He alone can give you peace and happiness. He is not called the Prince of Peace for nothing.

The issues of life and death are of far of greater importance and value to you than the gaining of material possessions, fame, power, and influence. True Christians are the happiest people on earth because they have made their peace with God Almighty. They have the joy unspeakable and the happiness that is beyond the reach of the monetary power. They are new creation on their onward journey to a sure and certain everlasting life. They have overcome fear and the power of the evil one: Satan the Devil by the precious blood of the Lamb and the words of their testimony (Revelations 12:11).

You can have these same privileges free of charge by coming to the Lord Jesus Christ and by giving your life to Him. I have been sent to offer to you this wonderful invitation of mercy to come and give your life to your God. Jesus is waiting on the portal at the entrance to the door of your heart and knocking. Please invite Him into your heart (Revelations 3:20)

Perhaps you are reading this book and you were once a fervent Christian, but the cares of this world and the deceitfulness of riches have lured you away from your Father God. Your love for your wonderful Saviour has gone cold and you have backslidden. You no longer feel the sweet presence of the Living Saviour Jesus Christ in your life anymore and The Father now seems so distant and unapproachable to you?

I have good news for you. The Father has commanded me to tell you to come back home to Him – He is waiting and watching, waiting, and watching for you with open and outstretched arms. He is the most wonderful and forgiving Father. Hear what His Holy Spirit says: 'Seek ye the Lord whilst He may yet be found; call upon Him whilst He is near ... He will abundantly pardon.' (Isaiah 55:6–7).

CHAPTER 8
WHO ARE THE CHRISTIANS?
PART 2

In the last Chapter we dealt with the question of who are the genuine Christians. We explained that the true Christians are only those who acknowledge Jesus Christ as their Lord and Saviour and are genuinely determined to follow Him and keep His holy law in spirit and in truth [John 15 vs. 14] [Matthew 7 vs.21].

We reiterated that anyone aspiring to be Christian must be prepared to be a beacon of light in the world of darkness and perversion and that the kind of life they live must reflect the faith they profess. We insisted with the categorical assurance of the word of God which says that unless our righteousness exceeds that of the Sadducees and Pharisees, we (Christians will NOT be allowed in the Kingdom of God) [Matthew 5:20]. Therefore, knowing the absolute holiness of God and the severity of His impending judgement against sin; we earnestly plead with those who say they love God to desist from sinning and serve the Lord with all their heart in purity.

In this chapter, we are going to continue to explore what the true biblical Christianity entails and who are legitimately the true Christians. The Christians people are a new creation of God drawn from all races, ethnicities, and nations. They are special people to God because of the blood covenant God has with His Son, our Lord and Saviour of the world. They are people with special relationship and intimacy with God; they are set apart for the glory of God. The Christians are given the Book of Instructions on how to live for God on the earth; the Book is called the Bible. The Christians are the only people who are promised the gift of the Spirit of God to guide, direct and lead them in dealing with real-life situations.

The Christians are the only people that are given a cast iron guarantee of a good life here on the earth and an eternal life here after. There is no other religion on earth or in heaven that is like Christianity: clean, clear, logical, and transparent – no hidden secrecy, no special qualifications, and no requirements for prior personal human achievement for membership. Other religions give rules and formulas to follow whilst Christianity is the only religion that gives us a person, Jesus Christ who loves us so much that that He died on the Cross. Other religions have tried to copy Christianity by producing their own books, but none has ever equalled the truth contained in the body of works that make up the Bible. None has been as authoritative in the description of the creation, the origin of man and the destiny of humanity. No other religious texts have been as descriptive, prescriptive, or as prophetic with absolute certainty as the Bible. The veracity and the eternal truth the Bible contains are still being discovered every day and validated by archaeological and genuine scientific discoveries. No wonder the Bible says 'for ever oh Lord your word is established in heaven" [Psalm119 :89]. Christians are the only people who are given the Spirit of God. All the other religions without exceptions have only the spirit of Satan and polemical self-deception. The religion of Islam which seeks to copy Christianity by creating its own religious text called the Quran, it is full of human conjectures, incomprehensible and a dubious moral code that starkly stands at variance with the true holiness of God and the true biblical injunctions on moral standard that are acceptable to the God Almighty. See what the Lord sets out as the basic standard code for human morality [Matthew Chapters 5 through to Chapter 7] on what is commonly called the Sermon on the Mount.

Christianity is the only religion that stands by its words: - no ifs, no buts and no uncertainties. The word of our God is categorical – you know where you stand with our God: 'the soul that sins shall die' He announced uncompromisingly [Ezekiel 18:4]. However, he that believes in me though dead yet shall he live, and he who lives and believes me shall live for ever [John 11:25]. No ambiguities here just plain speaking!

Christianity is a religion of fairness, justice, mercy, and absolute equality. Unlike in Islam where women are regarded and treated as vastly inferior to men and only perceived as sex objects and as property belonging to men, both in life and even in death; in Christianity women are totally equal to men: because in Christ, we are all brothers and sisters with equal access to God through Christ.

Furthermore, all are equal before God. The rich, the poor, the powerful, the Kings, the servants, the educated, the illiterates - all are bought by the precious blood of Christ, and all are equally saved by grace alone and nothing else but the grace of Jesus Christ the Son of the living God.

The Christians are the favourites of God, indeed because they are His children; the Bible calls them Priests and Royals [Revelation 5:10]

The royal status indicates the position of favour with God and their appointment as Priests shows spiritual intimacy and closeness to the Almighty God. The Christians have been given the promises of God for protection throughout their lives [Hebrew 13:5]; the promises of joy [Psalm 30:5]; the promises of peace [Romans 16:20]; the promises of good health [3 John 1:2] and the promises of prosperity [Colossians 2:2] and above all the promises of eternal life [Titus 1:2].

Maybe whilst you are wondering reading this book why are the Christians so blessed and highly favoured. The answer is very simple: Jesus Christ, the Son of the Most High God. Jesus sacrificed Himself for the sakes of those who believe in Him and follow His way.

If you are reading this book and you are not a Christian, but you would like to become one. Well, you are more than welcome, welcome to a life of wonders, a life of happiness, a life that has great purpose and a life at the end of which an eternal life is guaranteed. Please do not let this wonderful opportunity pass you by, take the plunge because you have everything to gain and nothing to lose.

CHAPTER 9
HAVE FAITH IN GOD

The Bible narrates the story that led the Lord Jesus Christ, the Son of God, and the Saviour of Mankind to say to His disciples they must have faith in God [Mark 11:22]. The disciples had just witnessed a public display of the power of God. They were very surprised to see the tree that the Lord Jesus Christ had commanded to wither on the previous day had in fact completely died to the core of its roots. Such display of power had never been seen before.

The Lord Jesus Christ the Saviour of the Mankind explained to them that if they (the disciples) themselves had faith in dealing with anything, nothing will be impossible for them. But to have faith in God, it is necessary in the first place to believe that He exists and that He is the rewarder of those who diligently seek Him [Hebrews 11:6]. In many instances of life when things become rather hard and difficult to bear, the tendency for all of us is to seek a solution within ourselves and when this is not enough, we then try to seek outside help from those who are close to us like family, friends, and relatives. However when these efforts fail to resolve the problems then panic sets in and the problems then get bigger and bigger leading to greater and greater anxiety.

When people find themselves under pressure, they tend to become desperate, and the decisions taken out of desperation are very seldom wise and helpful. This is the reason why most people find themselves in a vicious cycle of defeat and failure with terrible consequences and the life which had hither to been very good and sweet, has now suddenly and unexpectedly turned sour, the shine is gone, and life becomes unbearable. However sad this may be people do not turn to God because in most cases they do not believe He can do anything to help resolve their situation. As they did not have God in their lives before the problem began, they assume there is no way God could possibly be interested in their plight. Some believe they are not good enough for God because they have been taught that God only hears the prayers of good people.

My friends as you are reading this book, maybe you know somebody who has lived through these circumstances, or someone who is currently living through this dreadful season of life. Maybe you yourself are going through this difficult period of your life right now and it now looks as if there is no way out, no solution and no hope. This book is especially written for you, and I have good news for you, but this is not based on positive thinking or a motivational speaking: it is based on the solid word of the

Lord my God Jesus Christ the Saviour and redeemer of Mankind.

The Lord Jesus Christ the Saviour and Redeemer of Mankind said He did not come for the righteous but for those who are unrighteous [Luke 5:32; Luke 9:56]. This is because the healthy people have no need of the physician and medication, and the doctors are only for the sick and the infirm. The Bible says that as long as we live in this world of sin and godlessness, there will be unhappiness and the uncertainties of life will pose its problems with all its unpleasant consequences [John 16:33]. There is no living person who is entirely free from personal problems. Some problems are not directly our faults; they are part of the baggage carried over through family or ethnic backgrounds that are deeply rooted in our nurture like a disease transmitted through the genes. However, in reality, most of the problems we encounter are the products of our own creation. The choices we make produce consequences which can be very far reaching with devastating effects on our fortunes and our entire lifetime ambitions. In all human societies, it is common knowledge regrettably that common sense is in short supply because common sense is invariably not that common; that is why in a complex and bewildering world, we need the wisdom of God to enable us to navigate the intricacies of life.

Many slogans have been invented to explain away the human conditions and I am sure you have heard some of these supposed words of wisdom: words like 'fortune favours the brave' and 'God helps only the deserving' or

'God helps those who help themselves'. The truth of the matter is that not many of us are brave and practically none of us is deserving of God. The Bible says all have sinned and have come short of the glory of God [Romans 3:23] and that there is no one that is good, no not one [Romans 3:12, Psalm 53:3]. So, if you are not wise and you are not brave or deserving and yet you have problems that are beyond your capacity to resolve; is there any hope or help available for you?

Yes is the resounding answer! Jesus Christ the Saviour and Redeemer of the world says, 'come unto me all who are struggling and are heavy laden' and I will give you rest [Matthew 11:28]. Our Lord Jesus Christ further says learn of me and you will find peace for your soul [Matthew 11:29]. If you are struggling and you find yourself overwhelmed by the difficulties of life and you can find no answer or help to your pressing problem; I have a solution for you: take your problems to the Lord Jesus the Son of God and the Saviour and Redeemer of mankind.

By coming to the Lord Jesus Christ in faith you are guaranteed of help in the time of need because He has promised that anyone who comes to Him, He will in no wise cast out [ ]. You will not be the first or the last person that has ever come to the Lord in desperation to seek help and support in the hour of need; so, do not allow pride or the whispering of Satan to deter you from seeking help from God. Do not listen to the lies of the enemy of your soul Satan the devil telling you that because you are not worthy, God is not going to hear your prayer. This book is titled the Audacity of Grace precisely because the grace and mercy of God is available in abundance to those who call upon the name of the Lord in their hour of distress and trouble. No one, no matter how sinful is beyond the reach of the mercy of God.

The Bible says if you had faith the size of the mustard seed, you would be able to command the mountain to be moved and be dropped into the sea and it will be so [Luke 17:6; Matthew 17:20] because all things are possible for those who believe [Mark 9:23]. This means you can call on God for help no matter in whatever situation you may find yourself. God has promised never to leave or forsake those who call upon His name – indeed the Bible makes it clear that it shall come to pass whosoever shall call upon the name of the Lord shall be saved [Joel 2:32; Acts 2:21; Romans 10:13]. The Bible says the name of the Lord is a mighty refuge and the righteous run into it and they are saved [Proverbs 18:10]. To have faith in God is a great gain and it is a profitable enterprise you can undertake without any drawback or regret. Even if your present relationship with God is not good, you are still welcome to call upon Him for help and you are not disqualified from receiving the mercy and the love of the Almighty.

You can always repair your relationship with God even in the midst of your trouble. Please do not say I will call upon the Lord God only after I have mended my way with God. You see our God is not a man and He does not think or act like a man. He is a loving and genuinely kind-hearted God full of loving kindness. Contrary to whatever you may have been told, our God is not a vengeful, fault seeking, fault finding, and judgment orientated God.

My ways are not your ways says the Lord [Isaiah 55: 8-11]. You see there is no one who can love you the way God does or more than He does – and this includes yourself. The love our God has for you is truly stupendous and it is genuinely beyond description. Firstly, He made you in His wonderful image and He made provisions for all you will ever need for the rest of your life long before you were born. As if this great provision is not enough; He sent His Only Son to the world to redeem you. You see friends, of all the great wealth of all creations in all universes, heavens included as well as the trillions of Angels, none is more precious or more important to God than His own beloved Son, our Lord Jesus Christ and yet He surrendered Him to be crucified like the worst criminal and vilified because of you. What then do you think He would deny you in the face of what He had already done? What else could He have done that He had not already done? What else do you think He would withhold from anyone who truly seeks Him and calls upon Him for mercy? Nothing!

Jesus Christ the Saviour and the Redeemer of Mankind says there is no demonstration of love greater than this that man laid down his life for his friends [John 15:13]. So, there you have it, the love of God for you is so great that there is nothing He would deny you if you genuinely come to Him with humility even in the midst of your seemingly insurmountable problem. There is nothing too difficult for Him. The Bible says ask, and you shall be answered, seek and you shall find and knock, and the door shall be open unto you. For what man is there among you who if his son asks for bread will instead give him stone or if he asks for a fish will give him snake? "If you bad as you are, know how to give good things to your children how much more will God the Father give what is good to those who ask Him for help" [Matthew 7: 7 – 11]

This is a golden rule of God. Do you need God's help in your life? I have been sent to tell you as His servant that God your loving God who loves you very dearly is waiting to hear from you without any preconditions. No ifs, no buts, your God is waiting to bless you, He is earnestly waiting to solve all your problems whatever they may be and whatever might have caused them. You are more precious to Him than your problems – indeed, you are more precious to Him than your sin. Because of Jesus Christ, the road is clear for you to be truly reconciled with the God of love who truly and genuinely loves you even as you currently are. It is time for you to exercise your faith in God and sit back and watch in amazement the joy and the consequent results of putting your faith in the only true God. This is your opportunity to put God to the test and see whether or not God will prove Himself to be faithful. You have nothing to lose, give it a try – what are you waiting for?

CHAPTER 10
WHAT IS FAITH?
PART 2

In the last chapter, which is Part I of this subject, we dealt with the definition of faith from the Christian viewpoint and explored what constitutes faith as a statement of precepts and canons with rituals that govern the lifestyle of those who subscribe to a particular religion. We pointed out that biblical Christianity was different because it is the only religion that provides credible answers to all the questions that excite the human mind and solves the problems associated with explaining the mystery of life, death, and God.

We explained that faith is a guide that helps to navigate the intricacies of life and the importance of believing in a credible faith cannot be over emphasized. We maintain the fact that, not believing in any faith is in itself a belief and those who claim to have no faith at all, do in fact have a faith but only that their faith is based on nothing! It is impossible to maintain a neutral position in so far as God is concerned because there is no independent ground with God: [Luke 11:23, Matthew 12:30] those who refuse to serve the true and only one God would invariably instead serve something that is much less than God and that without any reward or joy.

In this chapter, we are going to concentrate on the purpose and functions of faith. Faith is not an end in itself; it is a means to an end: you acquire faith to guide you in your daily living and to help you navigate the difficult circumstances of life – in other words to help you make sense of your everyday life.

The Christian Faith is not just a set of beliefs it is a set of principles that shows who we are and what we are. What a person does is a reflection of who he is: a baker for instance is a man or woman who makes a living by baking bread and selling it in the marketplace. Indeed, in the past, the English people were named on the basis of their occupation: 'Mr. Smith is a man who works with metal and if he is in the gold trade, he will be called Mr. Goldsmith. It is the same in biblical Christianity. A Christian is somebody whose whole life is taken up and dominated by the principles and personality of the Lord Jesus Christ the Saviour of the mankind.

So, embracing the Christian faith implies that you are a practicing Christian whose life is governed in practice by the teachings and the lifestyle of Christ our Lord and Saviour. Biblical Christianity is not a religion practiced only by assertion – it is a practical religion. The Bible says it is of no use to claim you have faith in God without providing the proof of such faith by the demonstration of practical work [James 2:26]. Just as the nature of a man is revealed by his personality and behavior pattern, a true Christian is one whose lifestyle reflects the faith he or she professes. Jesus says it is by their fruit you would know them; a fruit tree is identified by the kind of fruit it produces – a good tree produces good fruit, and a bad tree produces a bad fruit [Matthew 7:20].

A question for you who are reading this book: who are you and who or what do you actually believe and follow? And if you say you are a Christian, what kind of Christian are you? Jesus Christ our blessed Lord and Saviour has made it clear that on the Judgment Day He will say to many nominal Christians, I do not know you. The Bible says many Pastors, Senior Pastors, Evangelists, Reverend Fathers, Bishops, Cardinals, Archbishops, General Overseers, self-styled Prophets, self-styled Apostles, Popes and whatever grandiosely arrogant title you choose to confer on yourself.

All these people will say to Jesus Christ the King of kings: 'Your royal majesty Sir, we have done many things in your name: we performed many miracles, we healed the sick, we built great church buildings, we had a massive following on the social media. We built mega ministries and published many Christian books in addition to our world-wide television evangelism. The King will declare to them and say 'I never knew you, depart from me you who practice lawlessness' [Luke 13:27; Matthew 7:20-23].

You may say this is too drastic why would the servant be sent to hell fire after he had served God on earth? You see our God is an impartial God and He is not mocked – whatever a man sows so shall he reap [Galatians 6:7]. The Bible says all our individual works will be tested by fire before God on the day of Judgment for quality standard. Many works that fall short along with their owners will be burnt in hell. Some will have their lives scarcely redeemed but their work will perish on the order of The Supreme Judge of the universes, the Lord and Saviour Jesus Christ [I Corinthians 3: 15].

If your current lifestyle is not in total conformity with the commandments and the will of God, then you are deceiving yourself whatever title you may have conferred upon yourself on the earth. If you are playing around with sin and there is no small or big sin: to God His law is indivisible. Jesus Christ the Saviour of the World has said very clearly that He had come to fulfill the law – all of them without exception [Matthew 5:17]. What the Lord Jesus did on earth the same He expects from all His servants to do and to the same standard of holiness.

So, there you have it, the question now for you is what kind of work are you engaged in at the present? Will your work pass the quality test by fire? Will you be able to stand before the Supreme Judge and pass the biggest test of your entire life, the test of eternity? So, what will your answer be? If you cannot categorically answer this question in the affirmative with absolute candor; then I must tell you that you are in a grave danger. You must stop whatever it is you are doing now and attend to this as a matter of utmost urgency; for what shall it profit a man if he were to gain the whole world but, in the process, loses his own soul in hell? You have nothing with which to bargain with Jesus in exchange for your soul. If the Holy Spirit is convicting you of any known sin in your life, this is the time to attend to it and seek forgiveness through genuine repentance and humility before God.

I am convinced the Lord is using this book to warn some of His servants and some particular individuals to start mending their way before it is forever too late to repent. Do not assume that because you prayed for the sick and they are healed in the name of Jesus; that that somehow makes you special, no, it does not. That you are given the gift of deliverance by the Holy Spirit so that you can in the name of Jesus perform miracles; this does not suddenly make you special in any shape or form – you are still just a sinner saved by grace and washed clean by the blood of the Lamb of God. You did not do any of these by your own special power. Therefore you deserve no praise, no honour, or special status – you are still just an unprofitable servant who has received the grace of his blessed Master.

All the glory and honour belong to the Lord Jesus the sweet Saviour of the world alone. Furthermore, He has the rights, power, and authority to award rewards to His servants as He sees fit [Matthew 20:15 - 16]. Our Lord does not have any, neither does He approve of celebrities [1 Corinthians 4: 7]. There is nothing unique about you that should make your head swell, let alone to make you think you are exempted from the life of piety and humility. Indeed, the more you are used by God, the humbler and more Christ centered you are expected to become. The Bible says today is the day and when you hear His voice of warning, harden not your heart.

I have been sent to reiterate that our God is still in the business of dispensing mercy and grace; but I am instructed to warn you that His justice, righteousness, and judgment still stand inviolate, so let everyone be warned and tremble. I am sent to clearly state that mercy and grace operate up and until the time of judgment but are not available afterwards. Please be warned!

You who are reading this book, I want to ask you a question in the light of what the word of God is saying: Now if the Christians will be judged for what they did in the flesh here on the earth so severely like this, where then do you think those who do not accept The Lord and Saviour Jesus Christ will be? The Bible says if the righteous are scarcely saved, where will the sinners be? [1Peter 4:18]. The Lord is speaking to your soul at this moment in time. Please do not turn away and reject the mercy of God. This is an urgent call of great importance in your entire life and your eternity. Your life and your eternity are now at a great risk, whether you know it or not.

Jesus Christ the blessed Saviour of the world is calling you to come to Him, He is pleading with you very tenderly and He is waiting for you very earnestly. Hear what the Bible says: Now is the day of salvation [2 Corinthians 6: 2]. Now is the only time that is certain for you, you really do not know what is going to happen to you in the next hour let alone in the next day. Come today to the Lord of your soul and offer yourself unreservedly and you will have a weight of sin and burden lifted from your shoulders. You will be assured of the everlasting life plus a life of peace here on the earth: one of the great names of our Lord is the Prince of Peace. This peace is available to you today, it is NOT the kind of uncertain and unreal fake peace the world dangles in your face but which it really cannot offer.

We are talking of a genuine long-lasting peace of mind and soul in this world and a guaranteed everlasting bliss in heaven. Come on then, jump in what are you waiting for? Please bow your head and say a short prayer in closing this chapter:

'Lord Jesus Christ the Saviour and Redeemer of the world; I have heard your word from your servant, I now offer myself and my life to you unreservedly, I accept that I am a sinner and receive Your forgiveness for my sin for which you died on the cross. Accept me into your Kingdom and wash my sin with your precious blood and make me yours for ever. Amen.'

If you have said this prayer with a sincerity of heart, then the Lord has accepted you into His Kingdom. You must now find an Evangelical Church near you where you can go and worship this wonderful God and Saviour Jesus Christ.

Make a Difference with Your Review and unlock the power of generosity

"The best way to find yourself is to lose yourself in the service of others."

— MAHATMA GANDHI

People who give without expecting anything in return live better happier lives.

So, let's make a difference together!

Would you like to help someone just like you—curious about living a victorious Christian life based on Grace but unsure where to start?

My mission is to make living a victorious Christian life based on Grace easy and fun for everyone.

But to reach more people, I need your help: most people choose books based on reviews. So, I'm asking you to help a fellow Christian by leaving a review.

It costs nothing and takes less than a minute but could change someone's Christian journey. Your review could help many people change their lives.

To make a difference, simply scan the QR code below and leave a message

CHAPTER II
TRUSTING GOD WITH YOUR PROBLEMS

> "Pursue, for thou shall surely overtake."
>
> — *1 SAMUEL 30: 8*

We are going to talk about life's setbacks and what to do when we are faced with the inevitable and shattering situation in our lives. In (1 Samuel chapter 30:8); the story of David and his men, we see what can happen even at the best of times. David a good and self-confident leader of 400 strong armed men. They were just returning from an expedition after a hard day's work, to their camp only to find that the camp had been sacked and burnt down to ashes. What is more everyone in the camp had been taken captive including the two wives of David. Furthermore, all their wealth has been stripped and plundered and the wives and children of David's men have been taken as spoils of war along with all their earthly possessions. The devastation of this calamity was such that the followers of David, about 400 men blamed

David for the calamity and were about to stone him and rebel against his authority. David had double catastrophes on his hands – the loss of his wives and children and a mutiny in his camp. The Bible tells us that David and his men were greatly distressed and reduced to tears – the defeat seemed total, and David and his men were at their wits end.

We all have such moments in our lives, a soul-destroying moment when all our strength and self-confidence evaporate under the crushing weight of heavy defeat. Everything that could be done had been done and stubborn problems refuse to shift. All hopes and positive thinking and planning have proved inadequate in the face of the cool reality that is practically beyond our control.

So, what do you do under such blistering circumstances? Do you throw the towel in and wave a surrender flag? Do you succumb to the self-defeating fatalistic philosophy of 'what will be will be' and comfort yourself with assurance that you have done your best? Do you convince yourself it is time to call it quits? If you are a Christian, you don't, certainly not! You turn to God, the source of limitless power, authority, and strength. You strengthen yourself in the Lord of your salvation. You call upon the God that never ever fails, a God that specialises in doing impossibilities, a wonder working God of ages.

This exactly is what David did. The Bible says 'David strengthened himself in the Lord his God' – the operative word here is the notion of personal God. Because David knew God personally as his God, he was able to call on

Him for help. The Bible further tells us that God answered David's prayer. David was directed to go after his enemies in the strength of God and recover all that the enemies had taken, including his wives, his children and all the wealth and the entire community that had been taken prisoners.

David prevailed because he took his setback to the only one God who could truly help him – the Almighty God. Many people facing unexpected difficulties of life would turn to any perceived solution but God. You see, to many people God is the last solution that they would consider – a last resort when all other alternatives have been explored and have failed. Is this the position you find yourself? Clearly there is no doubt that we cannot go through life without experiencing situations that are sometimes beyond our control; what you do in the period of crisis shows who you really are and your priorities in life. Who you turn to for help reveals where the focus of your life lies? Those who put their trust in the Lord know that our God is a formidable deliverer and a marvellous protector; to Christians therefore, God is not the last resort of protection and source of help – He is the very first port of call.

David instinctively recognised this truth. He called upon his God, and he was given the grace to do the impossible; he was not only empowered to recover his wealth and his community, but he also recovered his dignity, his position and his authority as an undisputed leader of his people. The enemy's (Amalekites) plan of destroying David's life and his reputation as a great leader failed because God was with David and God was with David because David called upon God with all his heart. Furthermore, had David not recovered what his enemies had taken from him and his followers and had he failed to restore his reputation, his destiny as the future King of Israel would have been put in great jeopardy – because who would want an incompetent and a known failure as King of a nation?

This is what happens when you learn to depend on God and when you take your setback to Him. Our God is a God of second chances. You see acknowledging that you are powerless is the first decision you need to take and confess before the Lord before you can secure victory through His power. Telling yourself and God that you are powerless is not the same as giving in to fatalism and hopelessness; it is a sign of humility before God and acknowledging that only by His intervention on your behalf could you succeed.

When you surrender to God, what you are saying is Lord I cannot handle this situation, but I know that only you can. God loves it when acknowledgement of human powerlessness is put before His throne in prayer of humility, because this represents an acceptance of God's sovereign power over all situations and circumstances. It is at this stage that the grace of God is released and the situation that at first looks indefatigable and insurmountable suddenly gives way and impossibility becomes possible. By grace, high mountains will be levelled, and crooked paths straightened. David trusted his God and he was given the grace to overcome and defeat all his enemies.

There was another servant of God who cried out to God in desperation because of his weaknesses; his name was Paul the Apostle. God told him 'My grace is sufficient for you, for my power is made perfect in human weakness' (2 Corinthians 12:9). I have been sent to tell you that God knows the limits of your strength and ability and that His grace is sufficient for all your needs all the days of your life. One more thing that you should know very well and take to heart; nothing ever takes our God by surprise and practically no one has ever gone far away as far to go beyond the reach of His grace and mercy.

Human mistakes and errors are nothing new to Him. Look at the story of the prodigal son. Having prematurely secured his inheritance, he moved far away from home, indeed as far as he could get in order to escape the scrutiny and the loving guidance of his father. He did not want to have anything to do with his father, he wanted to do his own things and he would not want his father telling him what to do now that he is now a big boy. At first everything was as he had expected, a riotous living free from moral responsibility. Life was good for a while, as money was flowing and so was what money could buy – temporary deceptive happiness. This went on for a while until the inheritance dwindled to nothing and the life of hedonism had to come to an abrupt end.

There were no more regular weekend parties as the good time friends and colleagues have now deserted, and as the bills started piling up with no visible means of paying them, the young man had to look for a job to pay his way. The first shock of his life was down on him. All his life he had lived under his father and on the family farm. He had acquired no skills or any competencies that could make him employable on the labour market. One after another all the employers he contacted had turned him down flat. With his fortune now gone, he was compelled to vacate his luxury apartment and moved out. He had at last managed to secure an employment with the pigs with the pig food as his wages! The young man had travelled a long way from a palatial family home to the luxury apartment and now arriving at the Pigs Pen. The young man has thoroughly undergone a salutary experience which has left an indelible mark on him.

One day he finally came to himself, he reasoned within himself that instead of continuing to eat pig food and living in a pig pen, maybe he could go back home to his father, ask for forgiveness and ask his father to take him back, obviously not as a son, because he had by then forfeited that rights: but this time as a hired labourer. One day you need to know that you will come back to yourself; meaning you will be compelled to face up to and own up to the outcomes and fruits of your wasted life. The Bible is very categorical about this truth – we will stand before God to receive the reward of our labour, whether good or bad. Our young prodigal son has come to the end of himself, and he was now confronted with the reality of his recklessness and godless living. With all his pride deflated and his cocksure bravado gone; he was left with the stark consequences of his rebellious and an ungrateful heart. He was unsure as to what his father would make of his defeated ego and shambolic and degrading appearance; but as he was left with no alternative but to swallow his pride and bear the indignities of having been a failure; he decided to take his chances with his father regardless of the worst possible outcomes. With this decision, he went back to see his father hesitatingly – who on seeing him from afar, went out to meet him. The father who had wondered about the whereabouts of the recalcitrant son and his welfare was only too glad to express his happiness at seeing him returning home. If he thought his father was going to reject him, he needed not have bothered as his father announced a welcome home party instead of the cold reception he was expecting; with fatted cow slaughtered to celebrate his return as the prodigal son.

This is how God treats anyone who on coming to their senses decided to return to God after they had gone away to pursue their selfish interest and subsequently found themselves badly battered by vagaries of life and its vicissitudes. Our God is willing and able by His grace to grant the request of any penitent sinner who with humility approach the seat of mercy and who want to start all over again and correct the errors of their past.

God wants you to bring your setback and your failures to Him and then to trust and have faith in Him to turn around your life just as He did for David. David depended upon the word of the Lord and by special grace pursued his enemies, attacked them and with power of God recovered everything that had been stolen from him and his people. Indeed, David recovered more, much more from the enemies than what the enemies had earlier looted from him and his people. The scale of David's victory against his enemies and the preponderance of David's spoilt of war was of such magnitude that he was able to bless other communities after having satisfied the material needs of his own community.

In other words, out of the surplus bounty of the spoilt of war recovered from the enemies, David became a source of blessing to others. Herein are the wonders of our God. When you take your problems and setback to God with humility and faith, your set-back will be turned around and you will receive beauty for ashes and double for your troubles.

Have you had a terrible setback in your life? Do you feel your life has been robbed of its destiny by the actions of the enemies in your life? Have you tried unsuccessfully to restart your life and you are not making any headway in restoring what has been stolen unjustly from you? Conversely have you been the worst enemy of yourself like the story of the prodigal son? Then why don't you come to God, the God of second chances. God gave David the second chance and restored to him more than what the enemies had stolen. God stands ready to do the same for you. Hear what the Almighty God promises to those who come to Him. I will restore to you the years that the locusts have eaten (Joel 2:25). If you come to God through Jesus Christ, the Saviour, and the Redeemer of the mankind you can be sure that the wasted years of your life will be restored. In this remarkable story, David recovered his reputation as a reliable leader of his people as his followers' confidence was restored in him. He later with his integrity unblemished became the most illustrious King of Israel. The grace of God is what you need for your life. The grace of God has the power not only to equip you for the present and the future; it can also cancel the negative impacts of the past and set you free for the rest of your natural life.

CHAPTER 12
PRAYER OF FAITH: THE WEAPON OF VICTORY
PART 1

Prayer of faith is the most powerful weapon God has given to Christians who love and serve Him. This weapon is also available to those who are yet to know Him but are desperately interested in knowing God. The Bible says the prayer of the righteous is very strong and avails much; (Proverbs 15: 29; James 5: 16). The reason why prayer is so powerful is because it was invented by God with a promise attached to it: "and you shall call upon me and I will answer" (Psalm 91: 15). In some other scriptural references, the Almighty says that when we correctly and satisfactorily walk with Him, He shall answer our prayer (Isaiah 65:24).

God is a good God of utter, unflinching, and unchangeable integrity, a totally faithful and awesome God who is unquestionably dependable and just in all His ways. The Bible says all His promises are yes and amen (2 Corinthians 1:20). This means, Christians are at liberty to call upon His name in prayer in the certain belief that their wishes that are in conformity with the wishes of God would be heard by God and answered.

Prayer as a weapon has been used to win a decisive battle in terrible wars where an insignificant army defeated a much larger and better resourced superior Army as in the war of the Midianites against Israel under the leadership of Moses the servant of God (Number 31:7) Prayer has also been used to change effectively the direction and hope of a backsliding nation back to God under the leadership of Prophet Elijah the great man of God (1Kings 18:37 38). Prayer has been used to remove generational curses and produced radical change and fundamental transformation from the life of failure and defeat into the life of achievement and prosperity (1 Chronicles 4:10). Indeed, the House of God - i.e., The Church building is called The House of Prayer (Matthew 21:13).

But what is prayer of faith? The prayer of faith is presenting yourself and your needs before God with solid expectation, reverential honour and with faith. Prayer in biblical Christianity is divided into three parts: the first part is an acknowledgment and recognition of who God is; the second part is the praise and worship that is due to His wonderful holy name because of the work that He has done; the third part is our petition – it must always be praise and worship first, an acknowledgement of the awesomeness of God and the praise of His wonderful name before personal petitions are presented before His throne.

We see this prayer sequence in the example given by our Lord and Saviour Jesus Christ, the Redeemer of Mankind. In Matthew chapter 6, verses 9 to 15, the Lord gives us a definitive template for a successful prayer life.

"After this manner therefore pray ye: Our Father who art in heaven, hallowed be thy name. Thy Kingdom come; thy will be done on earth as it is in heaven. Give us this day our daily bread. And forgive us our debts as we also forgive our debtors. Lead us not into temptation but deliver us from the evil one for Thine is the Kingdom, the Power and the Glory for ever and ever."

The Lord started with the acknowledgement of who God is as the Father, our Father who art in heaven. This starting up clearly denotes the kind of relationship that exists or should exist between God and us – a Father/child relationship - a relationship of mutual closeness, reverence, and love. What is the role of the father? It is one of caring, loving and protecting his children from danger and of providing for their needs. The father teaches, directs, and provides help to his children. The father supports, encourages, and stands solidly to fight the enemies of his children. However, with our God, nothing is impossible for Him. Our God has unfettered power, readiness, and the inclination to come to the aid of His children and to rescue them from all their troubles and tribulations.

Our Lord then followed the concept of the fatherhood of God up with the acclamation of adoration and worship – hallowed be thy name. Here the petitioner is asked to treat the encounter with God with honour and humility. David in the Book of Psalms says I will enter your Court with praise and reverence [Psalm 100: 4]. I will magnify the Lord of my salvation [Psalm 18:46]. It is only after the greatness and the reverential fear of God have been acknowledged that a request is then presented to God.

Here we see the kind of prayer that would be acceptable to God – 'Thy Kingdom come, and thy will be done on earth as it is in heaven'. Our prayer must be centred only on the will of God. This is essentially because only when the will of God is done in our individual life, that the blessing and the protection of God is guaranteed. What is the will of God? The Bible is very clear about what the Lord requires from His people: truth, justice and mercy to the poor, the weak and the widow and to love others as you love yourself (Isaiah 55:7).

Somebody asked our Lord Jesus the Saviour and Redeemer of the mankind, what is the greatest commandment? The reply came very swiftly: 'You must love the Lord your God with all your heart and secondly you must love your neighbours as yourself' (Leviticus 19:18). The implications of this sacred requirement are crystal clear: unless you love the Lord your God with all your heart and your neighbour as yourself, you cannot reasonably expect your prayers to be answered. Many people have been praying for years for blessings on their lives, but nothing has happened, yet they never bothered to examine their lives and their consciences to see what may be acting as impediments and blockages to their prayers.

Maybe you have been praying fervently to God over something for a very long time and your prayers have been met with failure as God has seemingly turned a deaf hear to your pleadings. Have you knocked and the door remained firmly shut in your face? Have you asked and failed to receive? I am sent to tell you that the hands of the Lord are not short or weak that they cannot save. Neither is your Heavenly Father deaf that He cannot hear your cry. What is more, our God is not blind, far from it, how can He who created the eyes and the sight be blind?

Maybe you need to retrace your steps; re-examine yourself and your lifestyle honestly and reappraise your relationship with God and the quality of that relationship. The Bible is very clear: 'If I regard iniquity in my heart, the Lord will not hear me' (Psalm 66:18).

The Lord continues to teach us in this prayer: 'Give us this day our daily bread'. Our daily bread refers to more than just our daily needs of food and drinks; it includes all aspects of our needs to ensure a healthy daily living. The Bible tells us the Lord our God is willing to provide us with all our needs in Jesus Christ our Saviour. In the Lord's Prayer, we are taught to ask for forgiveness of sin: 'forgive us our sins as we forgive those who sinned against us'. The Bible says all have sinned and have come short of the glory of God (Romans 3:23) Here we are required to forgive others who have offended us – whatever the gravity and the nature of the offence if we want God to forgive us our sins. This is another stumbling block that is preventing our prayer from being answered.

But if we forgive others of whatever offence they had committed against us, then we are free to ask the Lord for forgiveness for our own sins with the assurance that we will obtain His forgiveness. The Lord Jesus Christ asks His Father to 'lead us not into temptation'. This is very significant; why would the Lord ask for this? It is because there is temptation everywhere in the world. The purpose of temptation is to divert our attention and focus away from the path of righteousness and from the things of God.

Unfortunately, this diversionary tactic always works against our genuine interest. This is because our feelings and our inclinations are invariably wedded to sin and sinful desires. We are easily distracted because we do not retain the knowledge of God in our heart and God is not our sole focus. It is one thing for the Lord to protect us from temptation it is quite another for us to deliberately seek temptation for ourselves. Satan is the maker and promoter of temptations and his intention is always to destroy our joy, our lives and to circumvent the realisation of the will and purposes of God in our lives. So, if the Lord has delivered you from temptations, steer clear of the Satan's trap.

If you know you need deliverance this book is telling you where to go Jesus Christ the Saviour and the Redeemer of mankind is here and ready to set you free and you will be free indeed [John 8:36].

The Lord then askes that we be delivered from evil: 'deliver us from evil'. Temptations always lead to evil if we fall for it because temptations are evil personified! Both temptations and evil come from the same source: Satan and NOT from God. If you are delivered from temptations and protected from evil, then your life will be a shining example of God's mercy and blessing.

Friends the world is full of evils and wickedness, there are evils everywhere. The Bible talks of the evils that fly by night and the pestilences that go by day (Psalm 91). You don't have to go looking for evil, evil will of its own volition seek you out and come after you whether you like it or not. There are evils in the workplace, evils at home; there are evils in the street and they lurk around at every corner. Evils abound within the family, among the siblings and among friends; not to talk about the evils that naturally flow from the enemies: known and unknown.

This is the crux of the matter. It is very easy to avoid the evils coming directly at us from the enemies that we know and from the sources that are openly hostile to us. But what about the evils that emanate from the unseen sources and the unknown deadly enemies? How do you run from the enemies you do not know you have? Enemies that are infinitely stronger than you because they operate from the realm of spiritual darkness and from the pit of hell. Put simply, how can you on your own with your own little strength alone fight and defeat Satan the Devil? Impossible my friend! Jesus Christ our Lord the Redeemer and the Saviour of the mankind describes Satan as the strong man.

The Bible asks the salient question – can the captives of the evil tyrant be ever set free from his tyranny? The answer is no - because the victim is weak, and the tyrant is strong. Our Lord Jesus Christ the Redeemer and Saviour of the mankind says only the stronger man who can defeat the strong man and only when the stronger man has done so can he subsequently set free the captives of the tyrant. Satan is the tyrant and the strong man holding the weak humanity to ransom. Jesus is the 'Stronger Man' who has defeated Satan and his forces for ever and so He can save anyone who comes to Him for protection and mercy.

Do you have a problem that seems to persistently defy a solution? Have you tried everything within your power to no avail? Is there a mountain that seems impregnable standing in your way and blocking every vestige of success in your life? Then I have good news for you – try Jesus Christ in prayer! I have been sent to tell you that the Lord God still answers prayers and all His promises in the Lord Jesus Christ are yes and amen – meaning that your prayers said genuinely with faith in the name of the Lord Jesus Christ the Redeemer and Saviour of the Mankind will not be in vain. There will be an answer to your petition. Your Saviour is also your Redeemer and Deliverer and right now He is waiting to hear your petition.

All you need to do is come to the Lord Jesus Christ, there is nothing impossible for Him. It is necessary of course for you to give your life to Him. The Bible says if you did this God would in turn forgive you of all your sins and will remove evil pronounced against you (Jeremiah 26:13) and (Micah 7:19). Furthermore, the Bible further says God will fulfil the desire of them that fear Him, He will also hear their cry and save them (Psalms 145:19). "And therefore, will Jehovah wait that He may be gracious unto you; and therefore, will He be exalted, that He may have mercy upon you: for Jehovah is a God of justice; blessed are all they that wait for Him" (Isaiah 30:18).

Friends, the Lord's Prayer is designed for you to guide you, to lead you and to assist you in your daily life. The prayer of faith solves problems when it is directed at the true God. The prayer we are referring to here is prayer made to the living God, the true God of heavens and earth, and the Father of our Lord Jesus Christ, the Redeemer and Saviour of mankind.

The prayer of faith makes impossibility possible; prayer removes mountains, levels the valley and straightens the crooked path. If God can hear the desperate prayers of other people, He can also hear yours because no one is too far gone as to get beyond the reach of God's mercy. Call upon me in the day of trouble: I will deliver you and you shall glorify me.

(Psalms 50: 15; Jeremiah 29: 12).

CHAPTER 13
HOW TO PRAY AN EFFECTIVE PRAYER

In the last chapter, we talked about prayer being an effective weapon of victory for those who know and love God. We gave series of examples of the efficacy of prayer as wonderful weapon of victory. Jabez transformed a life of generational curse into a life of success and victory (1 Chronicles 4: 10); we read about how a small insignificant Army through prayer defeated a much larger and better resourced Army. We also talked about prayer as something God has committed Himself to because God is the one who set up the idea of prayer in the first place. We reiterated that prayer signifies our needs and our dependency on God. What is more, God likes to hear the prayers of His children. The privilege of prayer is by far greater than the actual presentation of our needs before God; it is an act of submission to His authority and sovereignty. It is recognition of His existence as our creator and the belief in His loving kindness.

In this chapter, we are going to continue with our study of the Prayer Template the Lord Jesus, the Saviour and the great Redeemer of the world gave to His disciples. Many people see prayer as a monotonous task that defies any sense of excitement. To some people prayer is something that only the Priests, Pastors and Evangelists do. Some people believe their prayer is irrelevant because there is no guarantee that God is going to hear let alone grant their request.

They believe because their lifestyle leaves much to be desired by way of holiness and religiosity, they conclude they are unqualified to approach God. Some believe the best approach is to seek the help of the Prayer intercessors. Whilst many of these differing reasons have degrees of validity – for example it is completely true that the Lord will have little regard for the prayer of somebody who harbours sin and hatred in their heart [Proverbs 28:9] and by contrast the supplication of the righteous man avails much with God [Proverbs 15:29].

However, God nevertheless wants everybody to come to Him in prayer. That is why the Lord Jesus Christ the Saviour, and the Redeemer of Mankind gave us The Prayer Template. How then are we to approach God in prayer? Is there a system or procedure we can employ that would guarantee us an access to God so that our prayer effort would not be in vain?

The answer to these two questions is invariably yes. Jesus did not just give us a prayer template He also taught us how to use the Template – how to approach God and get our desired results. There are broadly speaking two types of prayers: (1) There is corporate prayer and (2) private prayer. The corporate prayer is a group petition brought before the Lord on specific issues of interest to the particular group, organisation or nation. The family prayer session and collective church prayer requests come under this category.

The private prayer is the individual presentation of our needs to God on one-to-one basis. As the name implies, corporate prayer sessions are always conducted in public while the private prayer is conducted in private. Both types of prayers are legitimate and biblical, and the Scripture is full of examples of how God answered these two types of prayers.

When conducting private prayer, the Lord's instructions are specific and direct. We are to retire to a private room, shut the door and pray to God in secret [Matthew 6:6]. The Lord Jesus makes the promise that our Father who sees us in the secret place will recompense us for our effort. The individual private prayer in secret is an act of engaging in intimacy with God and one thing that private prayer does is that it deepens our relationship with God.

The more we pray, the closer we get to God, the closer we get to God, the greater our love for God becomes and the more we love God, the more we obey His will and commands and finally, the more obedient we are the more we are guaranteed positive response to our prayer. This is the truth because the key to answered prayer is obedience and humility!

The Lord Jesus Christ the Redeemer and the Saviour of Mankind says "if you abide in me (i.e., keep my commandments) and my words abide in you (as in reading your Bible regularly and learning the words of God) you will ask whatsoever you want, and it will be done unto you" [John15:7]. There is no promise stronger than this anywhere else, there you have it; the Almighty has spoken!

Now that you have decided to pray and be alone with God, you should relax and not be anxious. You should start with thanking God that you are alive to be able to talk to Him [Philippians 4:6]. Make sure you do not have dispute or quarrel with anybody [1Timothy 2:8] and that you have forgiven anyone who has offended you. You should follow this up with confession of your own sin before God and then ask for His forgiveness.

After giving thanks you should now proceed to make your request known to God [Colossians 4:2]. Furthermore, you must believe that all things whatsoever you have asked in prayer you will receive [Matthew 21:22] and thank Him in advance of having your request granted by Him in the name of Jesus Christ His only begotten Son.

How long then should you pray for and on how many occasions? There is no rule on the number of times you should pray and there equally is no rule about the length of time your prayer should take. The Bible tells us to pray without ceasing until our request is fully granted [1Thessalonians 5:17]. The Lord Jesus is our example of ceaseless prayer. He said that we should pray always and not give up [Luke 18:1]

The Apostle Paul, a formidable prayer warrior encourages all Christians to pray in every place lifting holy hands to God [1 Timothy 2:8]. We are encouraged to pray until we receive what we are praying for. Indeed, we should continue to pray even after we have had our request granted because the life of a man or woman does not consist mainly of material blessings. Pray for your health, family, your children, pray for your spouse. Pray for the future of your children and grandchildren. Pray for your community, pray for your Church and pray for your country. Pray not only for satisfaction of immediate needs and wants, pray also for long term needs. Pray that you might be protected from all evils. Pray for your Government and those who have authority over you. Pray in particular for the will of God to be done in your lifetime. Pray for revival for your nation.

The corporate prayer is a collective effort that comes in three different forms. The family gathering prayer meeting; the Church prayer meeting and of course a National Day of Prayer in defence of national interest. Having a corporate prayer meeting is an open declaration of the acceptance of God as the source of power and a solution centre. Corporate prayer is not only conducted in public domain, it can also be held in private. Thus, the collective prayer of the Apostles for the release of Peter from Prison in the Book of the Acts of the Apostles was held in private.

However, most corporate prayer meetings are held in the open with the public. King Solomon prayed at the opening and the dedication of the first Jewish Temple to God and God answered and granted his wishes (1 Kings Chapters 8 & 9). Prophet Elijah held an open prayer session during his battle with the Prophets of Baal and the Lord answered his prayer by sending down the fire to demonstrate who indeed the true God was (1 Kings 18: 36 – 38). On the basis of the scriptural evidence, it would appear that the corporate prayer is much more powerful than the private prayer.

CHAPTER 14
LIVING FOR CHRIST
PART 1

In this chapter, we are going to be teaching on what is expected in biblical Christianity from anyone who is a new convert to Christianity. The first thing that must be understood from the start is the fact that Christianity is radically different from all religions. Christianity is in fact not a religion at all in the sense that Judaism and all other religions are. Whilst all other religions teach good works as basis for determining the validity of devotion and the adherence to rituals as a means of identifying with the central tenets of the faith. Christianity on the other hand teaches that all the supposed human good works are totally unacceptable to God because all human good works are regarded as filthy rags before God (Isaiah 64:6).

Indeed, the Bible says, "all have sinned and come short of the glory of God" (Romans 3:23). The central teaching of Christianity is that man in his own effort can never ever reach the standard of God's holiness and righteousness that will make him acceptable before God. If it was possible for man to fulfil God's standard of righteousness, then the sacrificial and atoning death of Christ was done in vain. But we know Christ did not die in vain because the Bible says Christ died for the ungodly and we are all without exception in the eyes of God totally ungodly (Romans 5:6).

The other major point of difference is that whilst other religions like Islam see their deity as being distant and unapproachable, in Christianity God has issued a genuine invitation to His people to come unto Him (Matthew 11: 28). Christianity is a way of life of personal direct relationship with God Almighty. This personal relationship reflects the nature of the God of Christianity who desires to engage with His own people. Why does He want to do this? He wants to do this because He is an extremely loving God who wants a close and loving relationship with all His children. And this is yet another very important distinction of Christianity among all the religions of the world. Only Christianity regards God in such intimate term as the Father.

So, if you have just given your life to God as a new convert or you are one of the millions who are rediscovering the faith in God; then you need to know what God requires from you. God wants you to live your life for Christ in a loving relationship. God wants to be like a personal father to you with all that this entails. Jesus Christ the Saviour and the Redeemer of mankind has purchased with His blood, His life, His death, and His resurrection an amazing and unbelievable privilege of becoming son or daughter of God. Hear what the Bible

Says: "To those who believe in Him, He gave them power to become the son of God" (John 1:12)

If you become the son or daughter of God, it means God has taken the responsibility for your life, your welfare, your security, and your entire future. This is what living for Christ will produce in your life as you seek to know God more and become more intimate with Him.

CHAPTER 15
THE WORK OF THE HOLY SPIRIT

In the last chapter, we spoke about living for Christ. Christianity is an engaging active religion which emphasises having and maintaining a relationship with the Almighty God. This relationship demands that on accepting Jesus Christ as our Saviour and Redeemer we are expected to also surrender our lives to Him so that He can now become the Lord of our lives. This means our lifestyle both in public and private must become a reflection of His glory.

In other words, there must be an evidence of fundamental transformation in our mode of living and behaviour pattern that is consistent with the word of God as recorded in the Bible. We reiterated in that chapter that because unlike all other religions where human goodness or deeds of good work is highly rated and acknowledged, Christianity does not recognise human good works as acceptable before God. We quoted a direct reference from the scripture which categorically shows that human good works are nothing but filthy rags before God (Isaiah 64: 6). But does that mean that Christians are not expected to do good works? On the contrary, Christians are required to do work of righteousness that is far superior in quality and quantity than those performed by non-Christians because our God is a God of absolute holiness and righteousness. This is where the problems lie, the quality of righteousness demanded by God is far beyond what any human could by their own efforts ever aspire to achieve. This is the reason why Jesus had to come to the world and live a perfect sinless life and then make Himself a sacrifice for the sin of humanity. So now when a person gives their life to God through Jesus Christ, God forgives their sins and wipes clean the records of all previous sins. But that is not all, God now transfers all the goodness and the righteousness of Jesus Christ into the account of the new believer and that believer automatically becomes the righteousness of God – because they are now enjoying the holiness and righteousness that comes from Jesus Christ which is the only perfect righteousness and holiness acceptable before God.

When a person decides to give their life to God, they do so as a response to the invitation sent by God to all humanity. On accepting Jesus Christ into our lives, the Spirit of Christ enters into our lives, and it is this Holy Spirit that makes the salvation of God very real to us in our lives. As explained in the earlier chapter, the Holy Spirit just like the salvation given by Christ is made available to us purely by the grace of God – it is not something we can work to achieve by our own effort or receive as an entitlement.

Our Lord Jesus Christ the Saviour and the Redeemer of mankind promised to send the Holy Spirit when He was going back to Heaven to be with His Father God after having completed successfully and totally the task given to Him by God the Father of providing salvation for humanity and a final reconciliation with God the Father. It is this Holy Spirit who indeed is the third Person of the Holy Trinity, and He is our guide and our God. He is NOT a force or an expression; He is a genuine living personality. It is He who gives the believers the ability and strength to live a life that is in accordance with the biblical Christianity (Titus 3: 5).

The Bible tells us that we are saved by grace and not by our own works, but it is only a gift of God plainly and absolutely. It was all done by the Lord Jesus Christ the Redeemer and Saviour of Mankind (Galatians 2: 16). This grace of God has also made available the invaluable resources and power in the form of the Holy Spirit to help believers live a victorious and successful life. The Bible says categorically that Jesus Christ our Lord and Saviour was dependent wholly on the Holy Spirit of God and it was the same Holy Spirit that directed all His actions and ministry (Luke 4: 1).

Jesus Christ made a promise to His disciples that after His departure to His throne in heaven He would send the Holy Spirit who would permanently reside in His believers (John 14: 16 – 18). This promised Holy Spirit will confer power on believers; power that would enable them to do the will of God and would assist them in witnessing for Christ throughout the world. This Holy Spirit would not talk about Himself but would only be primarily concerned about Jesus Christ and His redeeming work.

There you are. As believers in Jesus Christ, you need the Holy Spirit not as an option in your life but primarily as a prerequisite, a fundamental necessity that is essential – indeed as essential as the breath you breathe that gives you life. In Biblical Christianity, it is totally impossible to be a strong practising believer without having received the Holy Spirit and it is equally impossible to serve the Lord faithfully without having received the Holy Spirit of God.

Today, the reason why it appears Christianity is on the wane is largely because those who call themselves the Servants of God have failed to seek the Lord faithfully and zealously enough and Christian nations especially in Western Europe and North America have collectively turned their back on God. You should not be like this, and the role of the Holy Spirit is to assist you to faithfully serve the Lord and actively avoid the ever-present danger of sliding back into ungodliness and life of sin.

The Holy Spirit provides not only the boldness necessary to proclaim the good news of the Kingdom of God, but He also provides a much-needed protection against the work of the enemies that seek to hinder the plans and purposes of God. The Holy Spirit holds the lines against

Satan and all his principalities and power of darkness so that Christians can go about their lives relatively unmolested and unhindered. This is why despite the massive opposition raised against the Apostles in the aftermath of Jesus' resurrection by the opponents of Christianity; the Apostles were not deterred as they grew in strength and boldness in preaching the Gospel of Christ in a dangerous and life-threatening environment. This ability and boldness were provided by the Holy Spirit. Indeed, such was their boldness that about 3000 people who heard the gospel preached to them accepted Christ and became Christians (Acts 2: 41).

Earlier on in the Chapter 2 of the Book of Acts of Apostles, we are told that the Holy Spirit came down from heaven and descended on the Apostles and they instantaneously became supernatural and superhuman (Acts 2: 1 – 4). This is what it means to be filled with the Holy Spirit; you will become supernatural and superhuman and this is what God wants to do for all the people who accept the Lord Jesus Christ as their Lord and Saviour. Once you have the Holy Spirit, then you have the Almighty God living in you. This is the reason why you need the Holy Spirit in your life to enable you to live for Jesus Christ a very successful and fruitful life.

CHAPTER 16
LIVING THE WORD OF GOD

We are going to continue to deal with the word of God which we started some chapters earlier. We see how important the word of God is and how powerful the effects of His word are in our lives. In the last chapter, we discussed the fact that words of curse spoken over somebody by those who had the authority over them could lead and indeed does lead to major difficulty for the person at the receiving end of such a curse. We have Jabez as an example of this phenomenon. Jabez suffered pain and rejection wherever he went because his mother had put a curse on him unwittingly by giving him the terribly name 'pain and suffering' because she had pain when she was carrying him in her womb.

We also see that just as Jabez cried out to God and was rescued when God changed his situation by overriding the curse imposed by his mother; so, would the Lord Jesus Christ, the true Word of God override the curse imposed on anyone who came to Him to be set free in genuine repentance. We intimated that our Lord Jesus Christ could do and does this because He has the supremacy over all creation both in heaven and on the earth. The word of God is an expression of the will of God; so, the word of God means exactly what it says – meaning if you are living according to the will of God; you will most certainly reap the positive and beneficial reward. The Lord Jesus said to those who were listening to Him that only if they allowed His teaching to influence their lives would they become His people (John 15: 14).

In other words, hearing and knowing His word is not enough: "if you hear my word, happy are you if you do them." Living within the word of God provides a great deal of protection to the believer and also provides guidance and light where guidance is desperately required (Proverbs 2; 6 – 8) 'For the Lord gives wisdom and preserves the way of His saints'. The Bible says the word of God is a lamp unto my feet and a light unto my path (Psalms 119: 105).

This means that when we live in the word of God, we let the word of God to determine and dictate the way we live our lives. Because the word of God is an expression of the will of God; we naturally find ourselves doing the will of God relatively effortlessly. When we allow our lives to be dictated and led by the will of God, we will invariably be surrounded by the awesome power of God in our lives. We would have an automatic protection and the blessing of the Almighty in whatever we do. Living in the word of God will open our eyes to the infinite possibilities of God's invincibility. This in turn will strengthen our faith in God and we will come to know that all things are possible for those who believe (Mark 9: 23). This is because with God the Bible says all things are possible (Mark 10: 27 & Luke 18: 27). We will then come to know the deep mystery of the Kingdom of God (Mark 4: 11). Living in the word of God leads to having more knowledge of God and knowing God leads naturally to loving Him as our God and Father. The Bible tells us that loving God makes all things to work together for good in our lives (Romans 8:28).

You who are reading this book, you can well imagine for a minute what would become of your life, if all things were to work simultaneously and smoothly for good in your life. No more fears of failure, no worries about what tomorrow might bring. No more obsession and trepidation about defeats and shame that comes from living a lifestyle of defeat and failure. No more fear of the enemies, seen and unseen; no more fear of Satan and all the power and principalities of darkness. This is what will happen to you if you who are reading this book would allow the word of God to guard your life and to lead you in your daily walk with God. He will give you the power to become more than conquerors (Romans 8:37).

Jesus Christ the Son of the Most High God is the Saviour and the Redeemer of the mankind and He is the Word. If you want to know more about Jesus Christ and how you can become part of His Kingdom, please contact us.

CHAPTER 17
THE IMPORTANCE OF THE WORD OF GOD

We are still talking about the Word of God. The word whether spoken or written has credibility depending on the source from which it emerged. The word of a poor drunken man does not carry the same weight as the word of decent and intelligent man. The word spoken or attributed to have been spoken by a King has a greater credibility that the one spoken by pauper. A word that proceeded from the seat of power is accorded much more weight and authority than those that emerged from lesser sources.

The critical factor deciding how a word is to be received or not received is wholly dependent on its source. Furthermore, the importance attached to the word received is in direct correlation to the perceived authority, position, and power of the speaker – even before the contents of the word are closely examined. The credibility of the word is further determined by the perception of the authority and the legitimacy of the source. Therefore, the word and the credibility of its source are closely intertwined.

The Bible tells us that the word of the Lord God stands for ever (Psalms 119: 89). The word of the Lord is a direct reflection of the integrity of God. In another Bible passage, we are told the word of the Lord will not return to Him void and that it would fulfil the purpose for which it has been sent (Isaiah 55: 11). God our God is a faithful, dependable God of unflinching integrity and perfect righteousness. His word is supreme with powerful creative force that burns up anything that stands in His way, and it is a massive destructive hammer that breaks in pieces every obstacle (Jeremiah 23: 29). The Bible tells us all that which we see today were all created not physically by hand but by the spoken word of God Almighty (Genesis 1: 1 – 25)

This understanding of the truth compels us to take a second look at the word of God as recorded in the Bible and to reappraise our attitude and our responses to how we handle the word of God. The Bible tells us that the word of God is living, and active and sharper than any two-edged sword, and piercing and even to the dividing of soul and spirit (Hebrew 4: 12). We can rely absolutely on the word of God because God takes very seriously His words; He said to Prophet Jeremiah,

> *"I will watch over my word to perform it."*
>
> — *JEREMIAH 1:12*

Furthermore, the word of God is a personality. The Bible tells us that "In the beginning was the Word and the Word was with God and the Word was God. The same was in the beginning with God. All things were made through Him and without Him was not anything made that had been made. In Him was life and the life was the light of men" (John 1: 1 – 4). This is a reference to the Lord and Saviour Jesus Christ, the great Redeemer of mankind. The word of God is not a sound bite like the empty words of the politicians – the word of Christ is Jesus Christ the only true Son of the living God.

It is a great source of joy and comfort for me to know that our God is such a God of unblemished integrity, and His word is completely reliable in all aspects of life. Why is this so very important? It is very important because you and I can totally rely on the promises of God as contained in His word. The word of God is sacrosanct, whatever God says He would do, that exactly is what He is going to do unfailingly. The word of God is not like the word of men – it is not a sound bite or an ordinary written record and covenants; the word of God is life, the word of God is a creative force, the word of God is Spirit, the word of God is truth, and the word of God is a personality.

This explains why the word of God is so powerful with creativity and righteousness because this same word of God is none other than the Lord Jesus Christ the Son of the Living God. "He was in the world and the world was made by Him and the world knew Him not" (John 1: 1 – 10).

So, Jesus Christ is the Son of God who transformed from being the Word of God into becoming the likeness of man of flesh in order to die for sinners and reconcile man to God. Jesus Christ the Saviour and the Redeemer of mankind was and is still the word of God in human form. God the Father has sent Him to the world to die as ransom for sinners: God did this to demonstrate His unbelievable love for humanity because there is no other way man could redeem himself from the quagmire of sin and ungodliness that has attached itself to humanity since the days of Adam and Eve.

The Bible tells us that the salvation and reconciliation between God and man which was purchased by the blood of Jesus Christ is available to all mankind. The Bible makes it clear that "God so loved the world that He sent His only begotten Son that whosoever believes in Him shall not perish but have everlasting life" (John 3:16).

If you are reading this book and you do not know God or His Son the Lord Jesus Christ, today is a good day for you. Maybe you have in the past heard about the Lord Jesus Christ and it did not make any sense to you at the time, then this book is for you. I have been sent to tell you that you need God's salvation that has come from Jesus Christ the Saviour and the Redeemer of the mankind. On the other hand, maybe you have never heard of the name of the Lord Jesus Christ before or still maybe you have vaguely heard of Him, and you thought at the time you had no time and no need for religion. I am sent to plead with you to reconsider your position in light of God's love and His unbelievable generosity in sending His Precious

Son to die a pitiless and painful death on the Cross. He who knew no sin and was perfectly holy in all His ways was condemned like a common criminal and unjustly executed with ardent murderers and wicked criminals – all because of you.

What then is going to be your response? Make no mistake; you can no longer plead ignorance because this book has been made available by God for your own sake. Failure to respond is not an option for you because you are henceforth responsible for your action before God. If you deny yourself of God's free offer of salvation and mercy, you will be held to account before God on the day of judgement.

The Bible makes it abundantly clear that those who deliberately refuse to accept the offer of free pardon and God's salvation are already condemned. Hear what the Bible says: "He that believes on Him is not condemned: but he that believes not is condemned already because he has not believed in the name of the only begotten Son of God. And this is the condemnation, that light is come into the world and men loved darkness rather than light because their deeds are evil" (John 3: 18 – 19).

CHAPTER 18
THE SUPREMACY OF CHRIST

In the last chapter, we dealt with the importance of the word. We said that word has significance in direct proportion to the credibility of its source. We explained that the word of a drunkard weighs less than the word of a respected professional in a high position of honour in society. We further explained that the word spoken or attributed to a king is accorded a much greater credibility and respect than those that came from the lesser sources. We concluded that a word received has a direct correlation to the perceived authority, position, and power of its source because the word and its credibility as perceived by the society is closely intertwined with its source.

Whilst man's word can be doubted with good reasons, the word that comes from God is of a completely different kind. The word of God is perfect because God is perfect, the word of God is supreme, because God is sovereign, the word of God is true, because God is truth. We then uncovered the open secret of the age – namely that this same word which has been with God from the beginning was indeed the great creator of the heaven and the earth and all the creation visible and invisible. We emphasized that this same word was transformed and became flesh in the likeness of the Lord and Saviour Jesus Christ the Son of the Most High God.

In this chapter, we are going to focus on the supremacy of the word of God over all matters and circumstances of life and death. As said above, Jesus Christ the Saviour and Redeemer of Mankind is the word of God personified. Word is much more than a sound bite; we use word as a medium of communication. Through words, ideas are conceived, generated, printed, sustained, and disseminated. The world as we know it today has been transformed by the word. Nations have risen and fallen because of the word; revolution has swept away a whole culture and old order because of the word. The word is very powerful, it is through the word that many people's lives have been moulded and transformed, some into greater and greater success whilst some others descended to the depth of defeat. Do not be surprised to hear that much more than you realise, your life is governed by the word, both spoken and written. The law that regulates your life is a written word and the system that determines your success or failure in life is based on the written words. However as explained earlier, in the real life, there is a hierarchy of word just as there is a hierarchy of power in terms of legitimacy, power and authority.

The word of the Lord is supreme because our God is sovereign and His word triumphs over all. Hear what the Bible says, "my word shall accomplish that which I please" (Isaiah 55:11). Both blessings and curses arose from the spoken word. Maybe you have been told you will amount to nothing in your life and a negative word of curse has been spoken over you.

A case in point is the story of Jabez. Jabez's mother gave her son a terrible name because she had experienced terrible difficulty and pain during his birth and so she named her son Jabez, which translates to 'pain'. The Bible says that "death and life are in the power of the tongue" (Proverbs 18:21) and because of this, Jabez's life was blighted due to the negative word of curse that was spoken over him from his birth. This curse followed Jabez everywhere he went until he could no longer carry the burden and he had to cry out to God for deliverance and said: "Oh that you would bless me and enlarge my coast and keep me from evil" and the Bible says because of his word of prayer, God answered his request (1 Chronicles 4: 9 – 10).

In other words, Jabez appealed to the higher authority of God to countermand the dreadful word of curse his mother had spoken over him. At last, the curse was broken and overturned. What is your condition today? There are many people who are reading this book whose lives have been blighted by the negative word spoken over them. People in authority over you in one form or another be it your teacher at school, your coach or your boss at work who took dislike you and spoke disparaging and negative word that has come to stay with you for such a long time – namely that you will not make it in life, that you will not amount to anything. You have had your courage knocked out of you and your aspirations destroyed because of a thoughtless word spoken over you to destroy your confidence and your destiny.

I have been sent to tell you that there is grace and mercy for you in the Lord Jesus Christ the Redeemer and Saviour of Mankind. He alone has the power to overturn your adversity and change your mourning into dancing just as He did for Jabez. He is a healer not just of physical body alone, but also of all circumstances of your life; He can send His word to heal your past, preserve your present and protect your future. The Bible says – He sent His word and healed them and delivered them (Psalms 107:20).

This is the audacity of Grace, and the Lord is here to hear and answer your heartfelt prayer and you have nothing to lose but you have all to gain. Jesus is the word of God who has supremacy over all things, and He will replace and repair all the negative words ever spoken over you and give you a new blessed and fruitful life.

CHAPTER 19
LIVING THE KINGDOM LIFE

In this chapter, we are going to talk about what living the Kingdom life entails. First, we are going to ask what is living the Kingdom life? The Kingdom life is a life lived in accordance with the will of God; a life lived solely to magnify the glory of God. This definition is very important because it beautifully encapsulates the plans and purposes of the Kingdom of God. The word 'Kingdom' is a hybrid word meaning 'The King's domain'. The kingdom is a geographical entity and governance system headed by a sovereign and absolute Monarch who rules by royal edicts and decrees. In the Kingdom, there are rules and laws to be kept and those who live in the kingdom are subjects not citizens.

You see in a genuine kingdom the Monarch is everything. How does one acquire the ability to live a kingdom life? This is a question worth considering. Jesus Christ the Saviour and the Redeemer of the mankind told a noble Jewish Rabbi called Nicodemus who had come to seek the way to the Kingdom of God. He was told that he must be born again in order to gain access to the Kingdom of God. (John 3:3)

The Bible says that Nicodemus was astounded by the word of the Lord Jesus Christ, and he wondered how a person of his age, could re-enter his mother womb and then subsequently be born again. Nicodemus was not alone in this lack of understanding regarding the requirement of the new birth - being born again.

In our days there is a confusion surrounding the concept of the new birth. First there are those who believe that once you become a Christian, you are automatically born again. But if believing alone leads to being born again, then Rabbi Nicodemus, a believer would automatically have been born again already and would not obviously have needed to come at midnight hours to seek information on the same subject from the Lord Jesus Christ. Clearly there is more, much more to be done after accepting Jesus Christ into your life before you can be given the grace of being born again.

Jesus Christ the Saviour and the Redeemer of mankind says that a man has to be born afresh or anew if he wants to enter into the Kingdom of God. But how does a man become born again? Our Lord the Redeemer explains that "that which is born of the flesh is flesh and that which is born of the spirit is spirit" (John 3:7). Now we know that man is made of flesh and that which is made of flesh can only reproduce flesh. So, a second birth becomes necessary in order to acquire the status of being born again. The Lord further explains that this second birth consists of water and the Spirit. This means that a man or woman professing faith in Jesus Christ as the Lord, Saviour and Redeemer must be baptised in the water and then receive the Holy Spirit before the process of rebirth can be completed (John 3:5). The importance of this process of rebirth cannot be over emphasized because the Lord Jesus is categorical by making it a pre-requisite for entering the Kingdom of God (John 3:5).

The baptism process is a physical indication of an inner spiritual transformation of the new convert. The water baptism is a symbol of being washed and being cleansed this is the reason why the traditional and biblical baptism involves immersion in which the new convert is plunged into the water and submerged under water momentarily before being raised up from the water in the name of the Father, The Son and the Holy Spirit. The confession of faith in the Messiah makes the anointing of the Holy Spirit possible.

John the Baptist tells the people of his days that although he baptises people to repentance, there is one greater than him present who would baptise not with water but with the Holy Spirit and fire. Listen to what he says: "I indeed baptise you in water unto repentance: but He that comes after me is mightier than I, whose shoes I am not worthy to bear: He shall baptize you with the Holy Spirit and with fire" (Matthew 3: 11). Here John the Baptist is talking about the fundamental purpose of the ministry of Jesus Christ, the Redeemer and Saviour of mankind.

Water baptism as the second step after the confession of faith towards salvation is important; however, the baptism of the Holy Spirit by invisible fire is the most important action that sets the process of fundamental and transformational changes in motion in the life of a new believer. This provides the zeal on salvation and can only be offered by the Lord Jesus. It is through the Holy Spirit sent by Jesus Christ that a new convert can become alive to God because the Bible says that "only those who are led by the Spirit of God are the sons of God" (Romans 8:14).

John the Baptist went on to explain what Jesus would do through His Holy Spirit in the life of the new convert: He would thoroughly cleanse the new genuine convert and burn up with unquenchable fire that part of the new believer's life that are unacceptable to God (Matthew 3:12).

Suffice it to say that in order to live a functional Christian life of the Kingdom, being baptised in the Holy Spirit is an essential pre-requisite. You can tell who really has been genuinely baptised in the Holy Spirit by the kind of life they live. When you see people, whose lifestyles are totally incompatible with righteousness and godliness and yet they claim to be born again you must know instantly they are not born again according to the scripture. In order to live the Kingdom life, which is a life of victory, success, happiness and God focused, you must be born again and be fully transformed.

This is the life that Jesus Christ purchased with His blood, His death and resurrection for you and me and it is as available today as it was in the days of the Apostles. This is a life freed from needless worries, fear of life, fear of death and fear of tomorrow – indeed fear of everything. Christ has come to put an end to a nightmarish life of fear and hopelessness.

CHAPTER 20
WHOSE SIDE ARE YOU ON?
EXODUS 32: 26A

We have so far discussed grace which God has made available in very large inexhaustible scale to humanity. But God does not force Himself on anybody. In every age, God has allowed people a free choice of action and decision. However, this freedom of choice comes with the responsibility for accountability. Everyone will be held to account before God for how they used the opportunity they are given. You could choose to serve the Lord and be on the Lord's side or you could deliberately choose to ignore His love and His law.

However, choosing to be on the Lord's side as recorded in Exodus 32: 26 is the wisest decision any man can make. What does being on the Lord's side entail? Generally speaking; being on the Lord's side is taking a position that may not be popular within the society, but it is in accordance with the will of God as revealed in the scriptures. In today's world, the prevailing culture of perversion and ungodliness coupled with the political correctness has meant that what in the past had been seen as wrong and unacceptable from the moral standpoint has now become not only tolerated but enthusiastically embraced.

The Bible says in the last days, people would no longer be able to accept good and sound biblical godly teachings, but they will become apostates believing the doctrines of lies and provoking God to anger. We can see from the scripture we have just quoted in Exodus Chapter 32:26 how the people of Israel responded. Having been liberated by the mighty hand of God from slavery of well over 400 years; witnessed the miraculous deliverance from the hand of the Pharaoh and his military machine; the opening up of the sea and the drowning all the forces of Pharaoh in the red Sea just so that the children of Israel could be protected from being driven against their will back into slavery. More than that, God in His bountiful provision had provided for all the needs of this people on their journey to the Promised Land. In the face of all these miracles and wonders, the Israelites chose to appoint for themselves a god of their own making. Whilst Moses was on the mountain talking to God at His invitation, they conspired together to force Aaron to create a new god formed from molten gold. They then proceeded to worship this worthless inanimate god and danced before it and gave it the glory that was due only to God Almighty.

As to be expected Moses on his return to the Camp of Israel found them dancing before this worthless god they had made for themselves; he therefore decided to ask the congregation to decide amongst themselves which of them were willing to be on God's side. In the end only the tribe of Levi volunteered to be on God's side - only one tribe out of twelve tribes that the Almighty God had taken out and set free from slavery took side with God! The rest had completely forgotten the blessings and the mercy of God so quickly that they were prepared to forsake and jettison the glorious, the most merciful and Almighty God in favour of the useless god of their own making.

I am sent to ask you the same question. What God of your own choosing or of your own making are you serving in place of the true and mighty God of Israel? The Bible prophesied about today's world where people would not be able to stand sound and godly doctrine anymore; they would reject the word of the Almighty and His merciful love and grace in favour of their own way and their own doctrine. Today there is a famine of the true word of the Lord in the world. It would appear no one is willing to preach the true and undiluted word of the Lord as bequeathed to the Apostles in the first Century.

In our days, the word of the Lord has become debatable, and Christianity has become a pick and mix religion. The notion and concept of sin, as defined by God's divine commandments, have become a narrative of subjective interpretation according to individual whims. The original biblical definition of sin is now a matter of personal opinion – in an age of supposed equal opportunity and fake political correctness, your opinion is as good and equally as valid as mine! Sin is no more abominable indeed some now wear it as a badge of honour. Recently here in London a Television presenter used his channel to announce to the world with fanfare that at the age of 57 after having been married for over thirty years with two grown up daughters that he had become homosexual. He did not bother to apologise to the wife he had deceived for many years, nor did he express any sorrow at all for the emotional trauma and anguish this revelation would undoubtedly cause his two daughters whose lives are now to be wrecked by this unbelievable betrayal, selfishness and recklessness of this unfair treatment. On the contrary, he announced how proud he was of his action – and true to form, all his colleagues on the Channel patted him on the back for his 'bravery' and 'integrity' and for 'coming out' openly and candidly. Nobody took any notice of the devastation this would mean for the wife he had treated very badly and deceived for over 30 years. Clearly there is definitely no sense of moral compass and the concept of right and wrong has been lost completely to this wicked generation.

But do not be deceived! God has not changed! His word on sin and judgement has not changed and will not change – no never! God's definition of sin remains inviolate; non-negotiable and it is NOT subject to human approval. Your opinion on what the Bible describes as sin does not matter because it is irrelevant. Every man and woman will be held to account whether they know it or not, whether they like it or not! You see, you will most certainly reap what you sow regardless of the prevailing self-deception of moral relativism and self-deluding ambiguities – you can assert your rights as loudly as you want and shout human rights from the top of the roof in protest. The Bible has made it clear that man is given to die but once and after that he will face the judgement of God. Furthermore, the Bible warns that the "wages of sin is death" (Romans 6:23); so, the only question that matters is this: are you on God's side? If the answer to this question is not categorical 'yes', then I have been sent to warn you most stridently with all the strength within my frail human body and to plead with you to please be reconciled with God and fall in line on His side. Only those who were on His side survived the dreadful judgement that followed the appalling sin of idolatry when in one single day some three thousand people were wiped out (Exodus 32: 28).

The Lord God will not clear the guilty (Exodus 34: 7) because the Lord our God is a jealous God (Exodus 34: 14). But for those who repent and accept His invitation to righteousness and mercy which is only available through the grace of His Son and Saviour the Lord Jesus Christ, their sins will be wiped away and they will be cleansed by His most precious blood. Whatever 'god' you have created for yourself, you must know this 'god' cannot save or protect you in the days of trouble. Many people think because they don't actually set up a physical hand-made god in the corner of their home and worship it like some idol worshippers do, therefore they do not believe they have an idol. But you don't have to set up a physical idol before you can be guilty of idolatry. Anything in your life that is given more credence and time than God is indeed your own self-made god. Some serve the god of addiction; they are addicted to sex, pornography, and alcohol; while yet others serve the god of greed, inordinate ambitions, drugs and criminal lifestyle and perversion. Which one of these is your god? You see all these man-made gods are not God. There is one true God who sent His Beloved Son to die for the sins of the world. His name is Jesus Christ because He alone is the Saviour and Redeemer of mankind (Matthew 1:21).

To be on God's side you have to accept the Lord Jesus Christ into your life because The Lord Jesus Christ is the only way to God, the truth and the life and no one can come to God except through Him (John14: 6). To be on God's side is to be on the side of total safety and protection from the wrath of God that will soon sweep through this world and bring it to an end so that the Kingdom of God can be properly set up. The Bible says those who accept the Lord Jesus Christ into their lives "will not perish but they would have an eternal life in God" (John 3:16). So, what are you waiting for? This world will soon come to an end; but even if the world does not come to an end, yours would most certainly come to an end when you die – and you would most certainly die at some point – and so what then? If you come to God now, you will have nothing to lose but your fetters of sin and instead inherit the eternal joy of salvation of God through the Lord and Saviour Jesus Christ.

SINNERS PRAYER

'Lord Jesus Christ the Saviour and Redeemer of the world; I have heard your word from your servant, I now offer myself and my life to you unreservedly, I accept that I am a sinner and receive Your forgiveness for my sin for which you died on the cross. Accept me into your Kingdom and wash my sin with your precious blood and make me yours forever. Amen.'

Now that you have finished reading the entire book, if you have enjoyed and benefited from the book, you can make a difference with your Review and unlock the power of generosity.

> *"The best way to find yourself is to lose yourself in the service of others."*
>
> — MAHATMA GANDHI

People who give without expecting anything in return live happier, better lives.

So, let's make a difference together!

Would you like to help someone just like you - curious about living a victorious Christian life of grace but unsure where to start?

My mission is to make Grace centre of living a victorious Christian life for everyone.

But to reach more people, I need your help: most people choose books based on reviews. So, I'm asking you to help a fellow Christian by leaving a review.

It costs nothing and takes less than a minute but could change someone's Christian journey. Your review could help many people change their lives.

To make a difference, simply scan the QR code below and leave a message.

APPENDIX

How many times have you persevered to the end of a play, or a television production, or a book, and wondered: Fine – so what happens to those characters *now?*

A lot of writers – in whatever medium – seem to take delight in leaving their readers dangling, wondering what to think, or where to go, or what to do next. Well, I say to you: there's no need to dangle here!

There follows a collection of Bible verses, quotations, and further prayers that may give you a solid footing to stand on. Far from dangling, you can now inspire and encourage yourself, in future days, by reading these collected snippets of wisdom!

If they help to *any* degree, then I've succeeded in part – but partial success is only partial. Ideally, I hope to have encouraged you to start your *own* collection of wise snippets. Material that you find for yourself will probably speak to you more powerfully than anybody else's selections.

As you move through the various periods of your life – as in fact you've already moved through several – such a self-selected collection will do more than any other consistent source to encourage and fortify you in your resolve to maintain your *serenity under fire*.

GRACE IS STRONG

> "The bridge of grace will bear your weight, brother. Thousands of big sinners have gone across that bridge, yea, tens of thousands have gone over it. Some have been the chief of sinners, and some have come at the very last of their days, but the arch has never yielded beneath their weight. I will go with them trusting the same support. It will bear me over as it has for them."
>
> — CHARLES SPURGEON, PASTOR AND AUTHOR

> "Once more, never think that you can live to God by your own power or strength; but always look to and rely on him for assistance, yea, for all strength and grace."
>
> — DAVID BRAINERD, MISSIONARY

> "When I hear Christians say, 'I don't do this, and I don't do that, and I am following a set of rules,' I immediately recognize that they know very little about the grace of God. They are trying to live the Christian life in their own strength. But Paul says, 'Be strong in the grace that is in Christ Jesus.'"
>
> — J. VERNON MCGEE, RADIO PREACHER AND BIBLE TEACHER

GRACE FOR TRIALS

> "Extraordinary afflictions are not always the punishment of extraordinary sins, but sometimes the trial of extraordinary graces. Sanctified afflictions are spiritual promotions."
>
> — MATTHEW HENRY, THEOLOGIAN

> "Grace tried is better than grace, and more than grace; it is glory in its infancy."
>
> — SAMUEL RUTHERFORD, THEOLOGIAN

> "God's silences are His answers. If we only take as answers those that are visible to our senses, we are in a very elementary condition of grace."
>
> — OSWALD CHAMBERS, AUTHOR

GRACE FOR HUMILITY

> "Good men do not always have grace and favour, lest they should be puffed up, and grow insolent and proud."
>
> — JOHN CHRYSOSTOM, EARLY CHURCH FATHER

> "All outward means of grace, if separate from the spirit of God, cannot profit, or conduce, in any degree, either to the knowledge or love of God. All outward things, unless he works in them and by them, are in vain."
>
> — JOHN WESLEY, THEOLOGIAN

GRACE, GLORY, HOPE, MERCY AND SALVATION

> "Grace is but Glory begun, and Glory is but Grace perfected."
>
> — JONATHAN EDWARDS, PREACHER, THEOLOGIAN AND MISSIONARY

> "The law works fear and wrath; grace works hope and mercy."
>
> — MARTIN LUTHER, PROTESTANT REFORMER

> "No man is an unbeliever, but because he will be so; and every man is not an unbeliever, because the grace of God conquers some, changes their wills, and binds them to Christ."
>
> — STEPHEN CHARNOCK, PURITAN CLERGYMAN

> "As heat is opposed to cold, and light to darkness, so grace is opposed to sin. Fire and water may as well agree in the same vessel, as grace and sin in the same heart."
>
> — THOMAS BROOKS, NONCONFORMIST PREACHER

> "Amazing grace! How sweet the sound, that saved a wretch like me! I once was lost but now am found, was blind but now I see."
>
> — JOHN NEWTON, HYMNIST

MORE GRACE IN THE BIBLE

> "And God is able to make all grace abound toward you; that ye, always having all sufficiency in all things, may abound to every good work: (As it is written, He hath dispersed abroad; he hath given to the poor: his righteousness remaineth for ever. Now he that ministe seed to the sower both

minister bread for your food, and multiply your seed sown, and increase the fruits of your righteousness;)"

— *2 CORINTHIANS 9:8-10.*

> "And he said unto me, My grace is sufficient for thee: for my strength is made perfect in weakness. Most gladly therefore will I rather glory in my infirmities, that the power of Christ may rest upon me."

— *2 CORINTHIANS 12:9*

> "For by grace are ye saved through faith; and that not of yourselves: it is the gift of God: Not of works, lest any man should boast."

— *EPHESIANS 2:8-9*

> "God, who foresaw your tribulation, has specially armed you to go through it, not without pain but without stain."-

— *C.S. LEWIS*

> "I have something which enables me to take it in the face of all the buffeting that comes my way, for I can always find resources that are adequate to take the knocks."
>
> — ALAN REDPATH

> "All outward means of grace, if separate from the spirit of God, cannot profit, or conduce, in any degree, either to the knowledge or love of God. All outward things, unless he works in them and by them, are in vain."
>
> — JOHN WESLEY

> "Do we approach God from a beggar's perspective or as His cherished child? If we have any difficulty seeing Him as our loving Father, we need to ask Him to help us develop a healthy Father/child relationship."
>
> — DAVID JEREMIAH

> "Cheap grace is the preaching of forgiveness without requiring repentance, baptism without church discipline, Communion without confession, absolution without personal confession. Cheap grace is grace without discipleship, grace without the cross, grace without Jesus Christ."
>
> — DIETRICH BONHOEFFER

> "Once I knew what it was to rest upon the rock of God's promises, and it was indeed a precious resting place, but now I rest in His grace. He is teaching me that the bosom of His love is a far sweeter resting-place than even the rock of His promises."
>
> — HANNAH WHITALL SMITH

> "Either sin is with you, lying on your shoulders, or it is lying on Christ, the Lamb of God. Now if it is lying on your back, you are lost; but if it is resting on Christ, you are free, and you will be saved. Now choose what you want."
>
> — MARTIN LUTHER

> "Oh, how very kind and good my heavenly Father has been to me! I have no aches or pains, no rheumatism, and now in my ninety-third year I can do a day's work at the orphan houses with as much ease and comfort to myself as ever."
>
> — GEORGE MUELLER

> "God doesn't just give us grace; He gives us Jesus, the Lord of grace."
>
> — JONI EARECKSON TADA

> "The best place any Christian can ever be in is to be totally destitute and totally dependent upon God and know it."
>
> — ALAN REDPATH

> "A state of mind that sees God in everything is evidence of growth in grace and a thankful heart."
>
> — CHARLES FINNEY

> "Your worst days are never so bad that you are beyond the reach of God's grace. And your best days are never so good that you are beyond the need of God's grace."
>
> — JERRY BRIDGES

> "Through many dangers, toils and snares, I have already come; 'Tis grace has brought me safe thus far and grace will lead me home."
>
> — JOHN NEWTON

> "A man does not get grace till he comes down to the ground, till he sees he needs grace. When a man stoops to the dust and acknowledges that he needs mercy, then it is that the Lord will give him grace."
>
> — DWIGHT L. MOODY

> "I am no longer anxious about anything, as I realize the Lord is able to carry out His will, and His will is mine. It makes no matter where He places me, or how. That is rather for Him to consider than for me; for in the easiest positions, He must give me His grace, and in the most difficult, His grace is sufficient."
>
> — HUDSON TAYLOR

> "The Cross is the lightning rod of grace that short-circuited God's wrath to Christ so that only the light of His love remains for believers."
>
> — A. W. TOZER

> "God specializes in giving people a fresh start."
>
> — RICK WARREN

> "Grace is not simply leniency when we have sinned. Grace is the enabling gift of God not to sin. Grace is power, not just pardon."
>
> — JOHN PIPER

activities.				
10. Is "on the go" or acts as if "driven by a motor".	0	1	2	3
11. Avoids tasks (eg schoolwork, homework) that require sustained mental effort.	0	1	2	3
12. Talks excessively.	0	1	2	3
13. Loses things necessary for tasks or activities.	0	1	2	3
14. Blurts out answers before questions have been completed.	0	1	2	3
15. Is easily distracted.	0	1	2	3
16. Has difficulty waiting turn.	0	1	2	3
17. Is forgetful in daily activities.	0	1	2	3
18. Interrupts or intrudes on others.	0	1	2	3

How to score

A diagnosis of ADHD depends on the type and number or symptoms your child is having and how those symptoms are affecting him or her. This screening tool is score by a healthcare provider and is used in the process of making a diagnosis. The tables on the back of this screening tool are for use by your child's healthcare provider. If you feel that your child may be showing signs of ADHD please complete this questionnaire and share the results with your healthcare provider.

For office use only (for health care provider interpretation)

IA Subscale raw score _____

HI Subscale raw score _____

Total subscale raw score _____

IA percentile score _____

HI percentile score _____

Total percentile score _____

%ile	5-7	8-10	11-13	14-18	5-7	8-10	11-13	14-18	%ile
99+	26	25	25	19	43	49	51	41	99+
99	25	24	24	18	42	48	50	40	99
98	22	21	21	16	40	42	47	36	98
97	21	18	18	16	37	37	38	32	97
96	19	17	18	15	36	34	37	30	96
95	17	17	18	13	34	31	35	28	95
94	17	15	16	12	33	29	34	27	94
93	17	15	16	11	30	27	33	26	93
92	16	15	16	11	30	26	34	25	92
91	16	14	15	11	29	26	32	23	91
90	16	14	14	10	29	25	31	23	90
89	16	13	14	10	28	24	30	21	89
88	15	13	14	11	27	24	30	21	88
87	14	12	12	10	25	23	28	20	87
86	14	11	11	9	22	23	26	20	86
85	13	11	11	11	21	22	23	19	85
84	13	10	10	10	22	22	23	19	84
80	12	10	10	11	21	21	22	18	80
75	9	8	7	6	18	17	14	13	75
50	5	4	3	2	10	10	7	7	50
25	3	2	1	0	6	5	4	3	25
10	1	0	0	0	2	1	1	0	10
1	0	0	0	0	0	0	0	0	1

For Healthcare provider interpretation only
Scoring sheet for girls

%ile	HI 5-7	HI 8-10	HI 11-13	HI 14-18	IA 5-7	IA 8-10	IA 11-13	IA 14-18	Total 5-7	Total 8-10	Total 11-13	Total 14-18	%ile
99+	24	20	18	19	23	21	26	21	38	39	43	35	99+
99	23	19	17	18	22	20	25	20	37	38	42	34	99
98	20	15	12	16	18	16	21	16	30	30	28	32	98
97	17	13	11	15	16	15	19	16	29	26	24	28	97
96	14	12	11	13	15	14	17	15	29	24	23	28	96
95	14	11	10	11	14	13	16	14	28	22	22	24	95
94	13	11	9	10	13	12	15	13	27	21	21	23	94
93	13	9	9	10	12	12	13	12	24	20	20	22	93
92	12	9	8	9	11	11	12	12	23	18	19	21	92
91	11	8	8	9	11	11	11	11	21	17	19	20	91
90	11	8	8	9	11	10	11	11	20	16	18	19	90
89	10	8	7	8	10	9	11	10	19	16	18	19	89
88	9	7	7	7	9	9	10	10	19	15	17	18	88
87	9	7	6	7	9	8	10	9	19	15	17	16	87
86	9	7	6	6	9	8	10	9	19	14	16	14	86
85	9	7	6	6	8	8	9	9	18	14	16	14	85
84	9	6	6	6	8	8	9	8	17	14	15	13	84
80	8	6	5	5	7	7	8	7	15	12	13	12	80
75	7	5	4	5	6	6	7	6	13	11	11	10	75
50	4	2	2	2	3	3	3	3	7	6	5	5	50
25	2	1	0	0	1	1	1	1	4	2	2	2	25
10	0	0	0	0	0	0	0	0	1	0	0	0	10
1	0	0	0	0	0	0	0	0	0	0	0	0	1

ADHD Rating Scale-IV: School Version

Childs Name: <u>Thomas Hockley</u>   Gender: Male/Female   Age: _____   Grade: _____

NHS No: <u>707 488 4197</u>

Completed by: _____   School: _____

Circle the number that **best describes** the student's school behaviour over the past 6 months (or since the beginning of the school year).

		Never	Sometimes	Often	Very often
1.	Fails to give close attention to details or makes careless mistakes in schoolwork.	0	1	2	3
2.	Fidgets with hands or feet or squirms in seat.	0	1	2	3
3.	Has difficulty sustaining attention in tasks or play activities.	0	1	2	3
4.	Leaves seat in classroom or in other situations which remaining seated is expected.	0	1	2	3
5.	Does not seem to listen when spoken to directly.	0	1	2	3
6.	Runs about or climbs excessively in situations in which it is inappropriate.	0	1	2	3
7.	Does not follow through on instructions and fails to finish work	0	1	2	3

> "My worth is what I am worth to God; and that is a marvellous great deal, for Christ died for me. Thus, incidentally, what gives to each of us His highest worth gives the same worth to everyone; in all that matters most are we equal."
>
> — WILLIAM CAREY

> "The future is as bright as the promises of God."
>
> — WILLIAM CAREY

> "Grace is the free, undeserved goodness and favour of God to mankind."
>
> — MATTHEW HENRY

THE AUDACITY OF GRACE
FINDING GOD'S SOLUTION TO YOUR LIFE'S PROBLEMS

"For by grace are ye saved through faith; and that not of yourselves: it is the gift of God: Not of works, lest any man should boast."

— EPHESIANS 2:8-9

This book book is for those who want to find God given purpose for their Christian life and the genuine strength given by the Holy Spirit to live their lives to the full effortlessly with confidence, joy and full assurance of glorious victory. The book focuses on the enabling, invigorating and all sufficient power of grace in the life of the believer drawing from the life of Noah as an example of God's grace.

The grace of God obtained exclusively through Christ is an all-encompassing, effective solution to all intractable physical, mental, social, psychological, economic and spiritual problems. A man or woman under grace is surrounded and protected by an invisible firewall of God's awesome providence and is therefore truly free from all alarms.

This book is therefore recommended for all who wish to find God's solution to all their lives problems.

About the Author

Pastor Stephen Bawa is the founder and Director of The Kingdom Ministries www.tkm.one and The Christian Television. The Ministry also broadcasts on the You Tube Channels: (1) Kingdomministries and (2) Ctv Uk.

Pastor Stephen Bawa was educated at London and Cambridge Universities. He is married to Linda Bawa and they are blessed with six adult children and eight grand-children.

Printed in Great Britain
by Amazon